"Having been through a number of minor earthquakes in California and Peru, I know that they last from a few seconds to a minute. Yet the death and damage spreads far from the epicenter and lasts for years—as seen in the Andean town of Yungay, whose entire population was destroyed and only a statue of Jesus Christ survived on a hilltop.

"This book vividly sets forth how an abortion that requires a relatively short amount of time is the epicenter of a deadly earthquake whose aftershocks spread far throughout the lives of the mothers, fathers, families and the whole of society. It personalizes a topic that many want to see from a distant, clinical, politically correct perspective, leading us beyond the news byte of abortion and motivating us to offer relief to the suffering victims. Reading it without tears is nearly impossible; responding to aid the many victims is imperative."

—Father Mitch Pacwa, S.J.
Host of EWTN Live

"This book is not just for your friends, co-workers, and relatives who still consider themselves pro-choice. That's because in Shockwaves, Janet Morana paints a clear, well-documented picture of how every abortion has a major ripple effect: a ripple effect that's more like a tidal wave leaving a path of death, destruction, and heartbreak. All of us, even those in the pro-life movement, need to be reminded of the ferocious fall-out of a so-called 'women's right to choose.'"
—Teresa Tomeo
Catholic Author, Journalist, and Talk Show Host

"This is a must read for those concerned about the fundamental moral tragedy of our time, and how much damage abortion does to families and our whole society!"
—Most Rev. James D. Conley, S.T.L.
Bishop of Lincoln

"Shockwaves will remain with you long after you've finished reading. Brilliantly argued, harrowing in its portraits of the walking wounded, Janet Morana has compiled a necessary and important book. By deconstructing our assumptions about abortion as a form of personal right, its morality, its function in modern society, how it actually works, Morana shows the tremor after the quake and arms us with what we need to know to prevent, prepare for, or survive the shockwaves of abortion. By cutting through a bedrock of harrowing true-life testimonies, Morana provides an indispensable resource."
—Theresa Burke Ph.D.
Founder, Rachel's Vineyard

"In her book, Janet Morana writes, 'There is no such thing as a private abortion,' and then provides overwhelming evidence to back it up. As a counselor to fathers of aborted babies, it warms my heart to see her include these all-but-ignored victims of abortion. Shockwaves will make even the most hardened pro-abortion activist reconsider the ramifications of so-called 'choice.'"
—Brad Mattes
President, Life Issues Institute

"In Shockwaves, Janet Morana brings together the wrenching testimonies of so many who have been devastated by the impact of abortion, starting with the babies and the mothers and rippling outward to fathers, grandparents, siblings, friends—to the abortion practitioners themselves. This compassionate acknowledgment of the extent of abortion grief will be an invaluable resource for healing."
—Maria McFadden Maffucci
Editor, Human Life Review

"The Gospel of Life is the Gospel of Mercy, and Janet Morana's Shockwaves will give you a deeper appreciation of how many different people need that mercy for every abortion that occurs."
—Fr. Wade Menezes, CPM
Fathers of Mercy Asst. General and EWTN Host

SHOCKWAVES
ABORTION'S WIDER CIRCLE OF VICTIMS

By
Janet Morana

CATHOLIC BOOK PUBLISHING CORP.
New Jersey

NIHIL OBSTAT: Rev. Pawel Tomczyk, Ph.D.
    Censor Librorum

IMPRIMATUR: ✚ Most Rev. Arthur J. Serratelli, S.T.D., S.S.L., D.D.
    Bishop of Paterson

October 7, 2017

The Nihil Obstat and Imprimatur are official declarations that a book or a pamphlet is free of doctrinal or moral error. No implication is contained therein that those who have granted the Nihil Obstat and Imprimatur agree with the contents, opinions or statements expressed.

Dedication

To Dr. Philip Ney and Marie Peeters-Ney, whose research and friendship made this book possible.

(T-933)

ISBN 978-941243-96-1

Copyright © 2017 by Catholic Book Publishing Corp., N.J.
Printed in the U.S.A.
www.catholicbookpublishing.com

Contents

Introduction

Janet Morana has put the reality of the myriad ramifications of abortion right in our faces and there can be no turning away. Abortion is not a decision made in the privacy of a woman's mind with her and her health care provider being the only players. No, like a pebble thrown in a lake that generates multiple, far-reaching, long lasting concentric waves, so it is with the death of one small innocent child. This book is most necessary to help us confront reality and look with courage on the devastated landscape of our world.

One can analyze abortion from many different angles. There is one which is not often mentioned; it is the angle of temporary insanity, of a dissociation from reality. One could in a sense consider all turning towards destruction and evil as a form of insanity, of leaving the reality of the world which God created. In 1979, Dr. Philip Ney, at the World Congress for Victimology and Holocaust survivors, raised the spectrum of a society composed of survivors of parental homicides. He coined the term abortion survivor. A generation was born which in order to survive needed to dissociate from reality. The living dead.

The only way to escape the horror of parents killing their children while in the womb is by dissociating from reality, escaping in the cyber world, using drugs, or allowing oneself to become a zombie, a clone just like everybody else. More recently as the downward spiral continues, a person loses being and identity with gender confusion and trans-humanism: "I do not know who I am, and I have no control over my life."

The only outlet for the anger is violence either fictive (video games and movies) or real (random killings and war) and living in a fog. Personal relationships do not exist at a deep level. The rupture with reality has deep implications which are only now beginning to become manifest.

The twilight zone world created by abortion has now become an obvious midnight scene.

Older people can mourn. They mourn in a deep guilt-ridden way. The burden of their guilt often overwhelms them and they choose death (euthanasia) as an escape from the pain. Younger people do not mourn in the traditional sense of the word. They are lost, the walking dead, guilty and angry with no words to express their unease. They themselves have been so dehumanized they do not know what grieving the loss of another human being could be like.

The ramifications of abortion are myriad and are like tentacles which have penetrated and destroyed lives, families, the medical profession and society as a whole. Janet Morana's book has the courage to examine and expose these ramifications. May we act on this warning before it is too late.

Marie Peeters-Ney

Marie Peeters-Ney is a pediatrician who worked in hematology-oncology in both Canada and France. After meeting Professor Lejeune in 1985, she joined his research team and worked with him on the metabolic consequences of chromosomal imbalances. Since 1992 Dr. Peeters-Ney has worked with her husband to train counselors throughout the world to deal with the damage caused by abuse and abortion. Together they founded IIPLCARR, now IHACA with branches in 27 countries.

Foreword

If insanity is losing contact with reality, Janet Morana is one of the sanest people I know. She not only takes the realities of abortion seriously, she responds to the multiple threats with intelligence and sustained effort. Her beliefs and behaviors line up well. And because the inner conflicts and disharmony of disparate ethics and efforts result in the futile expenditure of effort, by being consistently pro-life, Janet has plenty of energy. This she puts to rational, logical use in defending pre-born children and treating those deeply damaged by the many affronts of abortion. It is not surprising to find that in this book she writes about her beliefs and her efforts.

As she notes, Janet and I have known and worked together for some years. Though we don't always agree on philosophical and religious matters, we have mutual admiration and respect for what God enables us to do. Janet is secretary for the International Hope Alive Counselors Association (IHACA) and should be practicing and promoting the Hope Alive post-abortion and post-abuse method for it is empirically derived and outcome confirmed like no other program. I gently rebuke her for this inconsistency, but, note to the reader, this is the only one I know. I suppose like other effective medicine, people tend to avoid it because it doesn't taste nice. In fact it is really hard work. But that should make it more trustworthy; especially now that a version of Hope Alive has been developed for children that appears to be even more effective than the adult version.

In chapter 4 Janet describes abortion, chemical and surgical, for what it really is. You may want to skip this chapter. If it does not upset you, then something is very wrong, wrong in you. You have lost the capacity to empathize with the pain of babies and the horror and guilt of their parents. This is the dehumanizing that abortion is doing to almost everyone. The only remedy is to apologize to God for your apathy and promise that you will be more like Janet. You do not have an option.

You must respond to harsh reality with an all-out reasonable effort to stop the cruel killing of pre-born babies and learn how to become God-helping healers of deeply damaged families. This is the only way to remain sane.

It is about time that those who are concerned about the effects of abortion, include the deep damage to men. Once again Janet pulls no punches. Her careful description of typical instances should leave the reader enraged or weeping or both. Abortion has undermined the roots of the family. As a consequence of feeling powerless to stop the murder of their innocent baby, men leave their families and many millions of father-neglected children grow up very angry at all father figures and determined to take power into their own hands. Subconsciously they find revenge in killing the child of the man they have convinced they love and will be true to. So tragic history repeats and no one is the wiser, except a few like Janet who are determined to face the destructive reality of the most tragic event in human history.

Janet gives good examples of Post Abortion Survivor Syndrome, but nobody I know has plumbed the depths of this most destructive phenomena. Consider for a moment the reasonably deduced fact that about 50% of all humans in our world are abortion survivors. This means that at least half of humanity feel guilty for existing, cannot see a bright future, have few qualms about killing people since like themselves, they have no intrinsic value. It has become a very dangerous and desperate world with almost everyone bordering on psychosis. They cannot face the harsh reality of existence. Does that mean you should give up? Read on and Janet will help you understand why you must keep fighting the destruction of our species.

Janet does what each person who is really determined to face the harsh reality of abortion must do. She carefully includes the impact of abortion on everyone, well almost everyone. The only entity that rejoices in this calamity is Satan who has always wanted to thwart the deep desire of God to have trillions of mature, loveable friends. It seems Satan is winning, humanity will not survive. But no, God always wins. "In fact, unless that time of calamity is shortened, the entire human race will be destroyed. But it will be shortened for the sake of God's chosen ones" (Mt 24:22).

Finally Janet shows the depths of depravity occurring to once noble physicians and staff. They have murdered innocent small people and have no excuse. They have dragged the whole healing profession into the abyss with them for none of their colleagues are saying we must stop being hypocrites. This isn't evidence based medicine. There are no proper indications and no scientifically demonstrated benefits. In short what we are doing or condoning is criminal assault and we know it. God help us.

In her last chapter, Janet writes of the global effects of abortion. There is no doubt, with plenty of scientific evidence to back this assertion; abortion is the most pervasive, destructive, and damaging onslaught that humanity has ever faced. Just as true is the observation that people have never underreacted so badly. What is the matter with everyone, particularly Christians? How can they pretend such destructive effects from abortion as the universal exponential population implosion resulting in the economic ruin of every nation, will not put them out of work? God is not mocked. He so loved each baby He willingly died for every one of them. He will not tolerate the massive murder of His innocent babies. He never has.

When Janet is not so busy, she will use her well-earned credentials in Hope Alive group counseling to learn even more about the nuances of human hurt. Then she will need to write another book to inform you reader, just how depressing and terrifying it is to face the fact you killed or allowed to be cruelly murdered a beautiful, trusting, innocent, naked child. Will you have the courage of Janet to acknowledge your contribution to the destruction of yourself, your neighbor, and your species?

Oh my, Janet Morana, what have you done? Although you end this book with an optimistic note, the only sane conclusion is that all is lost. You brought all your readers to the edge of despair. "What must we do?" they say. I will reply for you. You must follow Janet's example if you wish to retain your humanity and sanity. And don't give her lame excuses. Surely if you are at all pro-life it requires a change of lifestyle, now not later. By becoming a Hope Alive counselor, you will see lives change and people grow. And don't worry about how much you will suffer from the epithets and alienation. You will be immensely blessed. That's a promised backed by God. Right Janet?

Philip G. Ney, MD, FRCPC, MA, Mount Joy College

Dr. Philip G. Ney MD, DPM, FRCP(C), MA is a psychiatrist who taught in five universities both in Canada and abroad. He is author of numerous books and scientific publications. In 1969 he coined the term abortion survivor and described the signs and symptoms associated with it. In the mid '70s he discovered the vicious interlocking transgenerational relationship between childhood mistreatment and abortion. He developed a counselling program, Hope Alive, to help those afflicted by childhood neglect/abuse and suffering from pregnancy losses. He has taught the group counseling Hope Alive in 40 countries. He has worked to help all those affected by the tragedy of abortion: health care professionals (starting the Society of Centurions), parents and children. His whole life he has felt duty bound to warn people of the terrible effects of abortion and euthanasia.

Chapter One

Abortion, No Big Deal; Not!

If you listen to the mainstream media you might think abortion is a necessary part of reproductive health care for women. The media and popular culture insist every woman must have a right to an abortion if she so chooses. But what does an abortion do to a woman's health and well-being? In this book, we will explore the physical and psychological damage caused by abortion, and, since every abortion results in the death of an unborn child, we will take a look at exactly what happens to the baby—the most innocent victim.

We also will take an in-depth look at the wider circle of victims, all of those who are impacted by the death of a child by abortion. Fathers, mothers, grandparents, siblings, aunts, uncles, cousins, friends, even abortion clinic workers and especially, the abortionists themselves. And finally, we will assess the impact on all of us, society as a whole.

No disease or natural disaster ends more lives than abortion. In 2015, the World Health Organization (WHO), a branch of the United Nations, calculated that the top ten causes of death combined were responsible for killing 25.9 million people worldwide that year. This list included heart disease, stroke, chronic obstructive pulmonary disease, lower respiratory infections, lung disease, HIV/AIDS, diarrhoeal diseases, diabetes, road injury, and hypertension. Natural disasters killed 60,000 and homicides were responsible for the death of another 490,765 people worldwide. Adding those numbers accounts for the deaths of more than 26.4 million people. The WHO also estimates that 40 to 50 million children die by induced abortion every year, which means more babies die before ever seeing the light of day than the top ten causes of death combined, plus natural disasters and murder. How did we get here?

Abortions have been performed since the beginning of time but only became widespread in the last century when the deadly procedure was legalized in many parts of the world. Legality bestows permission, which we can see taking place as more states and cities legalize marijuana. Lots of people smoked it before it was legal, but now many more people are smoking, eating, and drinking cannabis products. So while people who support abortion will argue that abortion has always existed, we can say with certainty that abortion rates would never have risen to these unfathomable levels had it never been legalized.

When abortion became legal throughout the U.S. in 1973, Americans began to see it in a different light. Many women I've spoken to during my decades of pro-life work have told me they would never have considered an abortion if it had been illegal. How did legal abortion happen in America? We can blame it, in part, on the 1960s and the giant generation known as the Baby Boomers.

In the 1940s and '50s, sex, for the most part, was contained within marriage. Adultery was rare and considered sinful by many. Then in 1960, the birth control pill Enovid was the first hormonal contraception method approved by the FDA. Married couples could now "regulate"—with great peril to the woman's health—the conception of their children. In 1972, the U.S. Supreme Court, in its *Eisenstadt v. Baird* decision, approved the Pill and other methods of contraception for use by non-married couples. The free love movement that characterized the '60s now had the sanction of the judicial branch of the U.S. government.

With the advent of contraception for all came what is now recognized as a "contraceptive mentality" that says: I tried everything I could not to conceive a child and it's not my fault that my birth control failed. It should be my right to have an abortion.

One year after *Eisenstadt v. Baird*, the right to an abortion through all nine months of pregnancy and for any reason was granted by the dual catastrophe of *Roe v. Wade* and *Doe v. Bolton*.

The logic behind the Supreme Court's decision to legalize the killing of pre-born children is based on two major fallacies: That abortion is safer than childbirth and that thousands of women were dying from illegal and botched abortions. The former assertion was based on junk science, and the latter was an outright lie.

First, let's discuss the claim that "abortion is safer than childbirth," which, interestingly, is still a favorite mantra of the pro-abortion community.

Clark Forsyth, senior counsel for Americans United for Life, wrote in the organization's "Defending Life: 2013" publication that the Supreme Court justices had very little medical information to rely on when deciding *Roe v. Wade* and *Doe v. Bolton*.

Forsyth wrote:

> *"The ultimate invalidation of state abortion prohibitions was driven by a novel medical claim—that 'abortion was safer than childbirth'—that had no reliable medical data (before or since) to support it. Since there was no record supporting this claim in either Roe or Doe, it was argued in the briefs and was directly disputed in oral arguments in both December 1971 and October 1972. Notably, no existing obstetrical textbook published before 1972 made or substantiated this claim.*

> *"The claim was based on a mechanical comparison of maternal mortality rates and abortion*

mortality rates using 1950s data from Soviet Bloc countries. Notably, this data consisted of raw numbers, not analyses from peer-reviewed or other reliable sources.

"... Ultimately, in the Roe opinion, the justices cited seven questionable medical sources to support the 'abortion is safer than childbirth' claim. All but one of these sources relied on the same 1950s data from the Soviet Bloc countries."

The second fallacy is the lie that helped change the view of abortion in the United States.

Prior to the *Roe* and *Doe* decisions, advocates for legalization began circulating the "fact" that 10,000 American women were dying annually in illegal abortions. Dr. Bernard Nathanson, the founder of the National Abortion Rights Action League—now NARAL Pro-Choice America—was among those spreading this misinformation to the media.

Years later, when Nathanson switched sides and became pro-life, he admitted he made this number up. The media then, as now, didn't do its homework, and began repeating this number as if it were gospel.

In a 2002 interview with *World Net Daily*, Dr. Nathanson said:

"We aroused enough sympathy to sell our program of permissive abortion by fabricating the number of illegal abortions done annually in the U.S. The actual figure was approaching 100,000 but the figure we gave to the media repeatedly was 1,000,000. Repeating the big lie often enough convinces the public.

"The number of women dying from illegal abortions was around 200-250 annually. The figure we constantly fed to the media was 10,000. These false figures took root in the consciousness of Americans, convincing many that we needed to crack the abortion law."

In addition to these fraudulent numbers was a misguided belief that making abortion legal would make it safe. Not for the baby, of course, because the desired outcome of every abortion is the death of an unborn child. But legalizing abortion was supposed to make it safe for the mothers of these blameless victims.

Just as abortion was legalized under these falsehoods, it was also presumed that those providing abortion services were trustworthy and respected members of the medical community. The reality is quite different.

Abortion clinics are allowed to operate as though they had just sprung up in a Gold Rush town. They are often unregulated and rarely inspected, staffed with people who have no medical training or advanced degrees, and helmed by abortionists who, with alarming frequency, have lost their licenses in one state and simply set up shop in another. The back alley has been moved to the front office.

In 2014, the *New York Post* revealed that New York State, the abortion capital of the country, was basically looking the other way where abortion was concerned. Under the headline, "NYC's tanning salons inspected more regularly than abortion clinics," reporter Carl Campanile wrote:

> *"The state Health Department is failing to inspect many of New York's abortion clinics—with some facilities escaping scrutiny for more than a decade, bombshell documents obtained by* The Post *reveal the following.*
>
> *"Health inspectors regulate 25 diagnostic and treatment clinics and surgery centers that provide abortion services—though pro-choice advocates say there are 225 abortion service providers in New York State.*
>
> *"Eight of the 25 clinics were never inspected over the 2000-12 span, five were inspected just once, and eight were inspected only twice or three*

*times—meaning once every four or six years. A
total of just 45 inspections were conducted at all 25
facilities during the 12-year period. By comparison,
city eateries are inspected every year and graded,
while a new law requires tanning salons to undergo
inspections at least once every other year."*

Tougher clinic regulations have been passed in many
states and they are routinely challenged by the abortion
industry—usually with Planned Parenthood leading the
charge. Some courts have ruled the regulations uncon-
stitutional and some have allowed them to be enacted.

One thing we know for certain is that a tiny woman
given too much anesthesia would have had a shot at
survival if Pennsylvania had building codes in place for
abortion clinics. When emergency personnel were called
to a Philadelphia "house of horrors" run by Kermit Gosnell in November 2009, they couldn't get a gurney in to
reach the unresponsive Karnamaya Mongar. She died,
and Gosnell is now serving a life sentence for her death
and the murders of three babies born alive after late-
term abortions.

Gosnell snipped those babies' spinal cords after they
were born alive and yet the secular media worked hard
to ignore his trial and conviction. I was in the courtroom
during his trial and on display was the filthy, antiquated
medical equipment seized from his clinic when the FBI
raided it. Also during the raid, investigators found the
bodies of aborted babies Gosnell had in the freezer and
the jars full of baby feet he kept in his office.

Interestingly, the raid on his office had nothing to do
with abortion: Gosnell was being investigated for illegal-
ly writing prescriptions.

The Gosnell case has led to several states enact-
ing laws regulating clinics. Common-sense things like
requiring abortion clinics to meet the same medical
standards as ambulatory surgical units and requiring
abortionists to have admitting privileges to nearby hos-

pitals. These laws have faced challenges by the same abortion industry that claims it is concerned about women's health.

In 2013, the Texas law HB2 was challenged by that state's abortion industry. This law required abortion clinics that have doctors who perform abortions to have admitting privileges in a hospital no more than 30 miles away. In addition, the law required that these clinics have certain standards like other ambulatory surgical centers, including hallways and doorways large enough for gurneys to fit through, an emergency generator to maintain power in the event of an outage, and sterilizing equipment. These are standard things you will find in other ambulatory surgery centers.

Amy Hagstrom Miller, an owner of some of these clinics in Texas, felt she could not make her clinics come up to these standards without it affecting her bottom line profit margin. So she filed a lawsuit that made its way to the Supreme Court. Miller contended these regulations would cause an undue burden on a woman seeking an abortion.

The Silent No More Awareness Campaign filed an amicus brief to the Supreme Court for this case, *Whole Women's Health vs. Hellerstedt*, which contained the testimonies of many women who were physically damaged at abortion clinics. These testimonies showed how the Texas law would prevent other women from experiencing similar problems by improving the conditions inside these clinics. Sadly, on June 27, 2016 the Supreme Court rendered its 5-3 decision in favor of the abortion industry, striking down Texas HB2. This was a sad day for women and for America, as the will of the people in the State of Texas was discarded. Similar laws in other states were also affected. So much for what our Founding Fathers intended for States' rights. The Supreme Court is rewriting the Constitution.

There is still some good news. Thanks to the pro-life movement and pro-life lawmakers, as this book was being written, 32 states had passed "Women's Right To Know" bills. Although these bills have been vehemently opposed by Planned Parenthood and the abortion industry, so far they have been upheld by court challenges.

These laws can require a 24-hour or longer waiting period between the time a woman books her abortion appointment and the procedure itself, and provide women the name of the doctor who is to perform the abortion, a description of the procedure, and scientific information about the development of her unborn child.

In states with few abortion restrictions, like Massachusetts, the needs of the woman receive very little consideration, and doctors who perform abortions have discarded the notion of a friendly bed-side manner.

Post-abortive herself and believing she was doing something to help women, Catherine Adair took a job in the largest Planned Parenthood in Boston. Read some of what she has to say about her experience:

"Working at the clinic I discovered that there was nothing pro-woman about abortion. Women were not counseled about their options. They weren't given any information about fetal development and if they asked any questions we lied to them. We spent very little time with them as we were told to get them into the abortion room quickly.

"We were told not to say the words abortion, fetus, baby or embryo. We told women the doctor would gently extract the contents of their uterus. Most of the women did not ask questions about the procedure or the baby. We were happy to keep them ignorant.

"Later I became a medical assistant for Planned Parenthood, and it was my job to get the women into the exam rooms and up on the table. When the doctor came in, if they were lucky, he would make eye contact with them. Minutes later, the doctor

would head off across the hall to kill another baby, and it was my job to get the patient into the recovery area as quickly as possible. Sometimes the women would be bleeding. Sometimes they would be fainting.

"After the abortion it was the nurse's job to look through the remains of the baby for what is called 'products of conception.' We used to joke and call them 'pieces of children.' This is the abortion industry. This is reproductive justice."

Catherine's experience is not an isolated incident. Many former clinic workers have left the abortion industry and tell similar stories. Patricia Sandoval, who worked at a Planned Parenthood in Southern California, remembers being instructed on how to refer to the unborn child: Never use the words baby or even he or she. If the child had to be mentioned at all, she was told to refer to the baby as "it."

On the Silent No More website *(www.silentnomore. com)* we have testimonies from thousands of women who regret their abortions, and many of them include comments about the way they were treated—or mistreated—at the clinics.

Victoria from Pennsylvania remembers her third abortion, performed at four months at a Planned Parenthood facility.

"My last abortion was done at four months. I felt there was no way out, I felt trapped. I was dropped off at Planned Parenthood, and went in alone, and petrified.

"At that abortion mill, I was told that 'it's the best thing to do, you won't feel anything' and it's only 'a blob of tissue.' The nurse escorted me to the 'procedure room.' The room was cold, with a distinct smell. While waiting for the pain meds to kick in, I saw in the corner a large canister with a long tube and attached on the end was a very sharp

object. Then I heard this sucking machine. The doctor took that tube with the sharp object attached
and shoved it up inside of me with such force that
I couldn't breathe. The pain medicine never kicked
in. I was crying, telling them the pain medicine
isn't helping, I felt everything. I begged the nurse
to help me, to stop. The pain was unbelievable! No
one listened. They just continued to suck my baby
through that tube into pieces."*

A woman who did not sign her name wrote a testimony about the day her daughter, whom she named
Natalie, died at an abortion clinic.

*"It was an old school building which seemed
sickly ironic, and we passed it once on the way
there. There were no picketers shouting at me or
mobs trying to barricade the door. Just one lone
voice out on the sidewalk drowned out by my sobs
and my boyfriend's yelling. We went through the
metal detector and up the stairs to the waiting
room. We sat there for hours, cramped into a room
with about 30 other women all waiting their turn.
One woman sat next to me and spoke loudly with
her friend about how she already had one son and
that was enough. It made me sad to think how
callous these people were, workers and patients
alike. I wanted so badly for some 'crazed, lunatic'
Christians to storm the doors and rescue me, but
they didn't come.*

*"I went in for my preliminary pregnancy test and
they confirmed that I was pregnant. But the nurse
told me things that I learned in later years were all
lies to get me to follow through with my decision:
like how it could be a tubal pregnancy (which is
extremely rare), or how, because I was so young, I
could die giving birth.*

*"When my name was finally called, a lump
caught in my throat. I signed in and went back
to the room where they do the suction abortions.*

I thought the doctor would be a nice person and take pity on me. He wouldn't even look me in the face, and was irritated when I resisted. I asked if it would hurt and he said, 'It's gonna hurt a lot more if you go through labor!' Dismayed, I finally gave in. What choice did I have? My boyfriend had driven me here and wasn't going to let me leave until I went through with it. I couldn't go home and tell my Dad, and it would become blatantly obvious in a few months what was going on. My baby's life ended that cloudy April day."

In throwing out the requirement for abortionists to have hospital admitting privileges, the Supreme Court is, in effect, helping the worst abortion providers to stay in business.

We can't know if an admitting privileges law in Maryland would have saved Jennifer Morbelli, but her story illustrates the tragic truth about abortion. Jennifer was a 29-year-old kindergarten teacher in Westchester County, New York. She and her husband were looking forward to the birth of their daughter, whom they named Madison Leigh. In her third trimester, their doctor informed them that Madison would be born with a seizure disorder, so the couple decided to abort.

Although there have been attempts to expand abortion access in New York, currently the procedure is only legal there up to 24 weeks. Jennifer, her husband, her parents, and her sister traveled to Maryland, where abortion is legal through all nine months of pregnancy. They sought the services of LeRoy Carhart, an abortionist who flew in to a clinic in Germantown and flew out when abortions were completed, to perform more abortions in Nebraska. Abortionists who travel from state to state are known to pro-lifers as "circuit riders."

On a Sunday in February 2013, Jennifer's abortion began with an injection of digoxin to stop Madison Leigh's heart, killing her. Laminaria, a type of seaweed, were inserted into Jennifer's cervix to begin to dilate it, so that in a few days, she would deliver a dead baby. Jennifer went to the clinic each day to see how the dilation was progressing. On Wednesday, Madison was delivered stillborn at 33 weeks, long past the point of viability. Carhart instructed Jennifer to rest at the motel until the next day, and he hopped on a plane bound for Nebraska.

When Jennifer started experiencing severe chest pain, Carhart could not be reached. Her family took her to Shady Brook Adventist Hospital in Rockville, Maryland, where she died the following morning. An autopsy would later determine that amniotic fluid had spilled into her bloodstream and prevented her blood from clotting. Jennifer and her daughter were buried together.

The damage that the abortion industry causes sends a shockwave that reverberates throughout the land. After Madison Leigh and Jennifer died, the shockwave reached all the way to a kindergarten class in New York. Her class lost their teacher; Jennifer's husband lost his wife and daughter; Jennifer's parents lost their daughter and granddaughter; Jennifer's sister lost her sister and niece, and the list goes on and on. Abortion reaches beyond the death of the baby. Many, many people are affected.

The undeniable truth is that making abortion legal did not make it safe. Many women have died from this legal, supposedly safe procedure. A partial list of women who have died from abortion can be seen at *www.silentno more.com/deathsfromabortion.*

But amid this ongoing tragedy, there are clear indications that life is winning: Abortion clinics have been closing in record numbers over the last several years. This is thanks to the hard work of many in the pro-life movement, especially my friends Troy Newman and Cheryl Sullenger at Operation Rescue; 40 Days for Life, and other groups and individuals who shine a bright light on the abuses in the abortion industry.

Chapter Two

The Wider Circle of Victims

Whether you consider yourself pro-choice or pro-life there are certain facts about abortion that cannot be disputed. I was never in favor of abortion, but for many years I didn't even realize it was happening. In 1973, when *Roe v. Wade* and *Doe v. Bolton* made abortion legal through all nine months of pregnancy for any reason, I was totally unaware. My mind was concerned with other things. I was in college in the early '70s and I watched as some of my friends were drafted into the Vietnam War. Some of these friends and neighbors came home in pine boxes. I wasn't against the war—I supported our troops—but yet I participated in some college protests. As far as the feminist movement went, I was hardly a radical. I supported women's equal rights to equal pay in the job market but there was no bra burning for me.

It wasn't until 1989 when I returned to practicing my Catholic faith that the abortion issue came onto my radar screen. In my parish, St. Charles on Staten Island, there was a new associate priest who preached on a regular basis about abortion. In fact, among the parishioners we would say "let's see if Father will use the 'A' word this Sunday." Of course the "A" word was abortion and the priest was none other than Fr. Frank Pavone, who in 1993 became the National Director of the pro-life organization now known as Priests for Life/Gospel of Life Ministries.

In October 1990 I accompanied Fr. Pavone and other pro-lifers from Staten Island to an abortion clinic on Long Island where there was going to be a "rescue." The Rescue Movement of the late '80s and early '90s involved groups of people sitting in front of abortion clinics, blocking the doors, sometimes even chaining themselves to the doors to prevent the clinic from opening, thus saving the lives of babies slated for abortion that day. Fr Pavone and I were there to pray in support of our friends and to counsel women about alternatives. If they were agreeable, we would take them to the nearby pregnancy resource center.

It was an eye-opening experience for me to see young girls with visible "baby bumps" on the way to taking the life of their unborn children. Some were escorted by a boyfriend and some by a parent. In one case the father of a young girl was literally dragging her by the wrist from the parking lot to the clinic. When he saw that the clinic was basically closed because of our rescue friends, he became very irate and started screaming at us. He obviously was forcing his daughter to have an abortion, to abort his grandchild. I can still see that young girl's face with tears in her eyes. This young girl had no "freedom of choice." They left that day and I will never know the outcome, but I have prayed for them.

That was it for me. I felt an invisible iron door close behind me and there was no going back. I was one hundred percent pro-life and committed to doing everything possible to help bring an end to abortion. While I was raising my three daughters, being a soccer mom, and volunteering with their schools for many activities, I made a shift in some of my own hobbies. I stopped going to ceramic class, quit the bowling league at the season's end, and even stopped teaching after-school religion classes. My spare time was now spent volunteering in pro-life activities.

Soon after this I began to encounter women who had had abortions and were seeking reconciliation and healing. Seeing these wounded souls, Fr. Pavone and I began to use the phrase "Abortion Hurts Women." We ordered special ink stamps and would stamp the phrase on all our outgoing mail. We encouraged others in our pro-life group to do the same. We also contacted Royce Dunn, founder of National Life Chain Sunday (held on the first Sunday in October) and asked if he would consider adding our phrase "Abortion Hurts Women" to be used along with their existing signs that read: "Abortion Kills Children." He agreed, and so at our suggestion the woman-centered message, "Abortion Hurts Women" began to be used in 1991.

Around 1995, Fr. Pavone and I met a Canadian psychiatrist who was a child and family therapist. Dr. Philip Ney also had researched extensively the damage that abortion does to women, men, and in fact, all of society. He has written many research articles and books, some of which can be found at his website *www.Messengers2. com.*

Dr. Ney also developed an abortion-recovery counseling program called Hope Alive and started a healing program for former clinic workers and abortion doctors called "The Society of Centurions" in 1997. Fr. Pavone and I were in regular contact with Dr. Ney and studied his programs. In fact, I am a certified Hope Alive counselor, and both Fr. Pavone and I are facilitators in the Society of Centurions rehabilitation program.

I continued to do pro-life volunteer work and in June 2000 I left my career as a New York City public school teacher and started working full-time for Priests For Life/Gospel of Life Ministries. Many of my teaching colleagues couldn't understand why I was leaving such a successful career and I assured them I would be helping them with job security. After all, if we continued aborting children, class sizes would diminish and some teachers would lose their jobs. I always find it ironic that the teachers' unions adopted a pro-abortion position when supporting political candidates.

I traveled extensively in my work at Priests for Life and met many women who shared their abortion experiences with me. In addition to Hope Alive, I was trained in the Rachel's Vineyard Retreat Program, which is an abortion recovery weekend retreat, and assisted on retreat weekends for several years. I heard first-hand the harm that abortion was causing to women—physically, psychologically, emotionally and yes, even spiritually.

In 2002, I developed and co-founded with Georgette Forney, president of Anglicans for Life, the Silent No More Awareness Campaign, which gives women who had been hurt by abortion a platform to speak publicly about their experience. After going through an abortion recovery program, these courageous women give their testimony in public places like schools, churches, banquets, and at the March for Life events worldwide.

The Silent No More Awareness Campaign has three goals. The first is to reach out to those hurt by abortion to let them know healing is available. The second aim is to reach out to women considering an abortion and urge them to choose life. The third goal is to reach those who are conflicted about abortion to show, through the voices of experience, the damage abortion does. These lived experiences trump all the rhetoric surrounding abortion.

In January 2003, as our nation observed the 30th anniversary of legal abortion, the Silent No More Awareness Campaign held its first public events. At various state capitols and in front of the Supreme Court on January 22, women held signs that said "I Regret My Abortion" and shared their stories of how abortion had adversely impacted their lives.

The raw honesty of these stories humbles me every time I read or hear them. Silent No More women and men confess in public the worst sin they have committed, and they do it, again and again, in the hope that they will help other women make the choice for life, and to reach people who are still lost inside a private prison of shame, grief, guilt and pain.

At *SilentNoMore.com*, we have compiled the testimony of thousands of these women. Here are a few examples.

Norma from California wrote about her six abortions:

"Someone might ask, 'Well, why would you keep going in to go get an abortion?' It was legal, and it was on the list of birth control. It seemed easy, it seemed harmless, and that's what they tell you. But I'm here to tell you, 30 years later, I suffered with the pain and regret of abortion. The kinds of things that I started to experience were hearing babies crying when I was sleeping, seeing blood crawling down the walls of my bedroom. I thought I was going crazy. Who sees that? Who? I couldn't understand it. I just couldn't, to the point where I wanted the visions to stop, so I wanted to kill myself. Every day I woke up with thoughts of, 'How can I kill myself? How can I put an end to this misery?'

"I was invited to a talk and I heard a lady give her testimony about her pain and regret of abortion, and I thought that was a weird story. Why would she be talking about that publicly? However, I knew that she was speaking the truth of what I was feeling, and what I was experiencing. For years I denied the fact that I had chosen abortions to end the lives of my children. I went six times into the abortion clinic, and ended the lives of six of my children. Why? Who would do that? I felt like a monster. I felt like God hated me. I felt like my husband hated me. I felt like my kids hated me.

"After hearing this lady's story as she stood up there and spoke so bravely about her abortion and the forgiveness of Jesus Christ, I knew I needed that. As soon as I went to the post-abortion recov-

ery group, God healed me spiritually, physically, emotionally, and mentally. I am here to say I will be silent no more, and I will tell my story boldly for anyone else who needs to hear it."

Leslie Blackwell, a regional coordinator for Silent No More in Richmond, Va., suffered for years from her two abortions, but it took her decades to realize the source of her pain.

"*We cannot live a lie...and live in peace! We must speak the truth, and the truth is that abortion has a profound impact on our lives.*

"*I know first-hand that the deep, dark secret of my two abortions kept me enslaved for over 30 years. The damages of unresolved guilt, grief, and shame played havoc on my personal life, but I never connected the dots. Like most people who've experienced abortion, I tried to bury the emotional pain and memories deep in my soul. I did my best to strain forward in motherhood, marriage, career, and community involvement. But my heart wouldn't settle—those abortions haunted me—and living a lie was killing me!*

"*Mounting research shows the emotional and physical effects of abortion on both men and women, including depression, substance abuse, eating disorders, anxiety, promiscuity, compulsions, risky conduct, and Post Traumatic Stress Disorder, as well as suicide and other self destructive behaviors. I fell in to most of those categories!*

"*It took years for me to finally realize I needed help and healing. In His perfect timing, God led me to a transforming weekend retreat that brought His love, forgiveness, and hope back in to my life. I was able to start moving forward, connecting the dots, and unravel my buried grief—and most importantly, I was able to give dignity and respect to my precious babies whose lives I took so many years ago. This is for you Timmy and Mary D."*

After being healed from two abortions, Mary in Minnesota was able to help a niece choose life for her baby. Here is her story:

"I had my first abortion at age 15 because an older friend of mine had a roommate who was raised by a single mom. He told me it was really hard on his mother and that he would've been better off if she hadn't had him. I don't remember much about my experience at the clinic. I think they showed me some video. Immediately after the abortion I felt numb. I got heavily involved in drugs and alcohol and further promiscuity until at 19 I got pregnant again. I went in to have another abortion and when I was in the exam room the doctor told me I was further along than they thought so I would have to come back the next day because the procedure was different. When the doctor went into another room to get something that she needed, I heard an audible voice say 'no.' When the doctor came back in I said I wasn't going through with it and left. This baby is now 33 years old and knows this story.

"I ended up marrying the father of this child. The marriage was tumultuous at best with numerous separations and reconciliations. After one eight-month separation and then reconciliation I found myself pregnant again. When I told my husband, he said he didn't believe it was his baby (it was) and he didn't care what I did about it. I ended up going in for another abortion. This time I went by myself and no one but my husband and I knew about it. I don't remember details of going to the clinic other than when I was driving myself home I became very light-headed and had to pull over on the freeway until I felt better (in the middle of the Lowry tunnel in Minneapolis). The marriage ended after seven years.

"I thought about my abortions over the years, but my attitude always was that it was a decision I made at the time and I had to live with it. I quit using drugs and alcohol when I got pregnant with my son, Rob. Without the self-medication I found myself very depressed. I was diagnosed with clinical depression in 1986 and spent three weeks in the hospital as a result. There wasn't any discussion about my abortions during this treatment or in subsequent rounds with different therapists. I believe I went to my pastor and his wife and told them (she was very involved in the pro-life movement). I was primarily interested in seeking forgiveness from God for what I had done. I had not yet made an emotional connection to what I had done and the resulting unhappiness I was experiencing. This includes numerous bouts of severe depression and wanting to die. I would not kill myself as I did not want my family to go through that grief, but I was dying on the inside.

"In 2001 I met and married a man who was the father of two aborted children and as a result he went through a healing program (Conquerors). He believed that I needed to go through some kind of program to help me deal with the issue as he thought that I was still suffering as a result. I went through the program and still did not feel any emotional connection. I wasn't able to grieve.

"A little over a year ago my niece, Angi, 22 at the time and unmarried, found out she was pregnant. We have always been close. She was going to use RU-486 to end the pregnancy. Angi was raised by a Christian mother and had walked away from her faith. As she was contemplating what to do she kept having my name come to her mind. On the Monday morning of her birthday week I sent her a text asking her to call me as I wanted to see her for her birthday. She told me when she woke up *and saw my text message she needed to call me. I told Angi my experience and how I had two babies that I chose to abort and how I almost aborted her cousin Rob. I told her that this was not just some tissue but a human being with a soul who deserved life. I promised I would help her in any way that I could. As a result, she decided to have her baby. I believe God sent her to me so that He could use my experience to save her baby and save her from the horror of having an abortion.*

"I went with Angi to her eight-week ultrasound. I was overwhelmed with emotion seeing that little heart beating. I had never seen this before. So ten years after the first healing program, I found myself inconsolable and convicted of what I did and the reality of those decisions. As a result I contacted Rachel's Vineyard and went on a retreat last May. It was very difficult and I was going to back out on several occasions because I did not believe I could face the pain. Instead I chose to claim God's promises that 'In my weakness He is strong' and 'His grace is sufficient for me.'

"I have for some time told Angi that if anything I have gone through could help her, the suffering was all worth it. I believe God intervened to save Kaenan's life and is also working to heal me. My hope is that God will use my experience to influence others who are facing an unplanned pregnancy and contemplating abortion as an option."

In 2004 we had our first man join the campaign and give his testimony in front of the Supreme Court at the March for Life in D.C. His sign read, "I Regret Lost Fatherhood." I will never forget his words. "How small of a man was I," he said, "that I let her go into that clinic to kill our child."

Also in 2004, the Campaign became international when Angelina Steenstra expanded our outreach to Canada and organized the first Silent No More event at the March for Life in Ottawa, Ontario, where women gave their testimonies of regret on the steps of Parliament Hill. Over the next few years, the Campaign expanded to Ireland, Argentina, France, Netherlands, Spain, Uganda, and Nigeria.

Since then we have been contacted by many women, men, and other family members seeking healing from the loss of a child to abortion.

This led to the Silent No More Awareness Campaign embarking in 2015 on a new initiative called *Healing the Shockwaves of Abortion,* based on the research and work of Dr. Philip Ney, whom I mentioned earlier, and the stories we heard from so many people involved in an abortion experience. We realized we needed to address what many referred to as the ripple effect of abortion grief.

Healing the shockwaves of abortion involves acknowledging the pain, allowing oneself to see the connection to the abortion loss, then healing that loss.

Well before *Roe v. Wade* in 1973, pro-abortion propaganda has emphasized that abortion is a woman's private, personal decision about her bodily autonomy. In the language of choice, abortion is spoken of as a personal and confidential health-care decision, and pregnancy is something that can be accepted or rejected. The enlightened, empowered woman facing an unplanned pregnancy steps away from the fray of opinion and politics, looks calmly at her life situation, her goals for the future, and decides if a child can fit into that scenario.

This distancing establishes an impenetrable boundary between the woman who is considering an abortion, or has experienced the procedure, and everyone else. The decision is hers alone. This strategy has proven to be a clever and very effective messaging campaign, which unconsciously has been absorbed by the majority of Americans. Even those who do not identify as "pro-abortion" are uncomfortable with the idea of interfering in what they see as a woman's personal decision.

But in the real world, far from the pro-abortion spin, abortion is not experienced as an isolated, autonomous decision of female empowerment—as if a pregnant woman is some sort of robot or isolated island. The reality is that a host of people are often intimately involved and quite influential in a woman's decision to abort. Though they may be disconnected from each other, all of those involved in the abortion decision and procedure remain deeply connected, emotionally and spiritually, to the child who dies in the womb.

Proponents of abortion often complain about the stigma that surrounds abortion, and they believe a greater affirmation and acceptance of abortion will remove the stigma. But the reality is that as we acknowledge and heal the impact abortion has on all those involved, we will finally dismantle the source of the stigma—unresolved shame and grief.

Real-life experiences are proving that many of us have been impacted by the premeditated death of an unborn child. If you compare an abortion to an earthquake, you can see that the unborn child is at the epicenter, as is the mother and the abortionist. That abortion, that earthquake, sends a shockwave that reverberates throughout the family and society.

The baby's father might have coerced the woman into having the abortion, or advocated for it, or paid for it. Or he may have opted-out, saying the decision was entirely up to her. Some fathers who want their children may find that even with begging, they are powerless to stop the abortion. Some fathers don't even know about the loss of their children to abortion for years, or ever. But the shockwaves reach these men, too.

Grandparents who tried to prevent the death of a grandchild, or who were active in encouraging their daughter to have an abortion, are also affected. Even those who didn't know about their daughter's abortion until years later feel the ripples of pain in acknowledging they lost a grandchild or grandchildren to abortion.

Children who lose siblings to abortion are touched as well when they discover that someone is missing from their family portrait. Aunts and uncles lose nieces and nephews to abortion. Cousins lose childhood playmates who could have become lifelong friends.

Everyone reading this book who was born after 1973 escaped the fate of one-third of those conceived after *Roe v. Wade*. Your life was not legally protected and you could have been aborted for any reason. You are an abortion survivor, as are those, like the pro-life activist Melissa Ohden, who actually survived an abortion attempt. Maybe you survived a selective reduction, but you lost the twin who was sharing the womb with you. There is no question that you have been touched by the shockwaves of abortion.

Ultrasound technicians who reveal the child in the womb to a pregnant mother are touched by the shockwave when the mother chooses abortion, as are people who may have driven a friend to the abortion clinic or paid for a sister's abortion. Those who encouraged abortion or just stood silent can be impacted, along with health-care professionals, counselors, teachers, or ministers who had a role in an abortion decision or procedure.

Many of those involved with an abortion experience will want to flee from the emotional fallout of the event as quickly as possible, but the truth is that abortion triggers a series of powerful physical, emotional, mental and spiritual *shockwaves*.

Think of what happens before, during, and after an earthquake. Along fault lines in the earth's crust, rocks under great stress shift violently, causing shockwaves to spread out in every direction. Sometimes these shockwaves can be felt by people thousands of miles away.

With abortion, the "fault line" is the conditions that made ending the life of the unborn child seem like the right choice. The violent shift takes place in the abortion clinic, where a child is literally torn from what should be the safest place on earth. The shockwaves of that abortion extend far beyond the epicenter of the procedure.

The physical, spiritual, and emotional trauma the mother feels changes her and how she interacts in all her relationships, present and future. But all those closely associated with the abortion decision, procedure, and aborted child can also experience a variety of after-shocks. The thoughts, loss, feelings, and memories from the event are often relegated to a distant, dark corner of the soul. This repression is common and can lead to depression and anxiety, anger issues, addictions, and difficulties in marriage and family relationships.

The good news is that the gentle but powerful waves of grieving, forgiveness, and healing are stronger than the destructive shockwaves of abortion. This shockwave phenomenon has been studied and researched by Dr. Ney for more than four decades. His term for the shockwave is "wider circle of victims."

Not convinced that these "shockwaves" exist? Then read on as we will take a look—starting at the epicenter and then radiating outward—at the shockwaves abortion generates and how they impact people's lives. Then we will talk about how all of us who have been wounded can find healing from the damage and devastation of abortion.

Chapter Three

Death at the Epicenter

The outcome of every abortion is the violent death of the most innocent victim: an unborn child. Let's take a look at the unborn child and what makes that child a welcomed child, wanted child, or an unwanted-and-then aborted child.

I gave birth to my first daughter Jennifer in 1978, and back then if you missed your period and wondered if you were pregnant, most doctors would wait to see you until you skipped two periods. Ultrasound was a relatively new invention and was not used routinely like it is today. In fact, I didn't know Jennifer was a girl until she was born. And even stranger, in light of everything we know today about life inside the womb—two years later my twins weren't discovered until I started my ninth month!

Today, many mothers want to know the sex of their baby as soon as possible and they see their baby on several ultrasounds before delivery. In fact moms, dads, and grandparents start showing those ultrasound pictures around to their friends even before the baby is born. I'm sure everyone has seen these photos on refrigerators, framed on desks, and of course, they are the first pictures added to the baby's scrapbook.

Ultrasound makes it hard for abortion supporters to argue that the unborn child is somehow not fully alive. But the evidence for this living, growing, unique human being can be seen long before the first ultrasound appointment.

A ground-breaking DVD called "The Biology of Prenatal Development," produced by The Endowment for Human Development and distributed by National Geographic, describes in incredible detail—with images from inside the womb—what takes place from the moment of fertilization until birth. According to this video, which provides a scientific perspective, "the dynamic process by which the single-cell zygote becomes a 100 trillion cell adult is perhaps the most remarkable phenomenon in all of nature."

Following fertilization, or the joining of the egg (oocyte) and sperm (spermatazoan) a new single-cell organism called a zygote is formed. The word means "yoked" or "joined" and the zygote is "the unique first edition of a new individual complete with a genetic blueprint."

Within 24-30 hours, the zygote has completed its first cell division. This cell division continues as the zygote completes its journey through the fallopian tubes. At six days after fertilization, the zygote begins to embed itself in the inner wall of the mother's uterus. By 10 to 12 days past fertilization, implantation is complete and the cells on the periphery of the zygote give rise to the placenta, which will nourish this "new individual" throughout the pregnancy. According to the Endowment for Human Development, "The life support systems of the placenta rival those of intensive care units of most hospitals."

Three weeks after fertilization, the brain begins dividing into three sections, and the respiratory and digestive systems begin to form. By three to four weeks, the heart emerges and grows rapidly. Three weeks and one day after fertilization, the heart begins to beat.

Week four is characterized by rapid brain growth. The heart beats 113 times per minute. Five weeks in, the cerebral hemisphere of the brain appears. This is where thoughts, memories, speech, vision, hearing, voluntary movement, and problem-solving begin. Early reproductive cells and hand plates develop.

Six weeks after fertilization, spontaneous and reflex-ive movements are noted. The ears start to take shape and primitive brain waves are detected. By six-and-a-half weeks, distinct elbows and hand movements can be seen.

How developed this unique human being is, often before his mother knows she's pregnant! If this preg-nancy is unexpected or unwanted, this is often when the abortion decision is made. No one who watches the embryology film could ever talk themselves into believ-ing this child is a mere clump of cells.

Let's continue considering this remarkable unborn child.

By the seven-and-a-half week mark, the ovaries are detectable in females, the eyelids are growing, and the fingers are separated. Also, the brain is highly complex, the fetus can roll over, bring his hand to his face, rotate her head, move his jaw, point her toes, and make grasp-ing motions. Seventy-five percent of fetuses will exhibit right-hand dominance by this time.

By eight weeks and two days, the bones, joints, and muscles closely resemble those of adults. This marks the end of the embryonic period and the beginning of the fetal period, which will continue until birth. The single-cell organism created after fertilization now has nearly one billion cells and 4,000 distinct anatomic structures—90 percent of the structures found in adults. Lightly touch-ing the embryo at this stage elicits a squinting response.

At nine weeks, the baby begins to suck his thumb, can grasp an object, sigh, stretch, and respond to light touch. In females, the uterus has become identifiable.

A burst of growth marks the transition from nine to 10 weeks, with the fetus increasing his body weight by 75 percent during this time. The baby can yawn, roll her eyes, and open and close her mouth. Fingernails and toe-nails begin to develop, and the unique fingerprints that will identify this particular human being throughout his or her life are present.

The nose and lips are fully formed by 11 weeks, and by 12 weeks, which marks the end of the first trimester, the entire body of the fetus, except the back and top of the head, responds to light touch. Also, bowel movements have begun.

At 14 weeks, females exhibit noticeably more jaw movement than males and in a departure from earlier weeks, stimulation near the mouth prompts the fetus to turn toward the touch, with an open mouth. This is the earliest sign of the rooting reflex that helps a baby find his mother's nipple to breastfeed. It is at 14 weeks that many doctors do more extensive tests and special ultrasounds followed by blood work. At this point parents can find out the sex of their baby if they choose to know ahead of time.

So many couples want to know the sex of their baby that a new trend has popped up: The "Gender Reveal Party." This is where a couple invites friends and family to a special celebration and when dessert is served, they cut into a cake to find a blue or pink interior—not natural colors for a cake but a clear indication of just who is in the womb. Most couples announce the name they have chosen for their new son or daughter during this gender reveal party.

There is a downside to the tests performed at 14 weeks and beyond: Fetal abnormalities like Down syndrome, spina bifida, cystic fibrosis and other problems can be diagnosed (or often, misdiagnosed) by this point and it is when many doctors will "counsel" the couple about termination, a.k.a., abortion. It's tragic that a wanted child's life could now be in jeopardy.

Between 14 and 18 weeks, mothers begin to feel stirring in their womb as their rapidly growing babies move around. Many moms describe this as a fluttering sensation.

By 19 weeks, the heartbeat begins to follow circadian rhythms that follow a roughly 24-hour cycle in response to light and darkness. The fetus will respond to a growing range of sounds by five months. Many moms begin to sing to their baby and of course the baby hears his parents' voices—hopefully they are pleasant voices; no yelling or fighting please! I started speaking to my children and my grandchildren when they were in utero.

At 22 weeks, considered the age of viability, the lungs have the capacity to breathe air. Fetuses can blink at six months, and the startle reflex is observed, particularly in females. By six months and three weeks, the brain is growing rapidly.

The eyes can produce tears at 26 weeks, and pupils respond to light at 27 weeks.

By now, all components for the sense of smell are operational. Also, introducing a sweet substance into the amniotic fluid leads to more swallowing, while a bitter substance causes the fetus to swallow less. Changing facial expressions and somersaults are some of the new skills developing at this time.

High- and low-pitched sounds prompt a response at 28 weeks. Two weeks later, the central nervous system becomes increasingly complex. By 32 weeks, true alveoli, or air pockets, form in the lungs. They will continue to grow until a child is eight-years old.

By 35 weeks, the fetus has a firm hand grasp. At 38 weeks past fertilization, the fetus sends out estrogen to initiate labor. And soon our baby will begin the journey down the birth canal to make his or her grand entrance.

So that's how we all began—welcomed, wanted or unwanted. But after reading this you might be asking, how does abortion fit into this baby picture?

Avoiding Pregnancy through Drugs

Appreciating the development of the unborn child will help us understand the variety of ways abortion is used to end the developing life, starting with the earliest-acting of the abortion-causing, or abortifacient, drug: the morning after pill, also known as Plan B. This is billed as a quick and painless way for young women who have had unprotected sex to avoid pregnancy. But how does it work? Let's take a closer look.

Emergency contraception comes in two forms, each employing a different drug. The so-called morning after pill uses levonorgestrel and it must be taken up to 72 hours after unprotected intercourse.

Levonorgestrel is not a benign drug. It is dangerous to the women and girls who take it. According to the website *www.drugs.com* women are cautioned against using levonorgestrel if:

• *They are allergic to any ingredient in levonorgestrel.*

• *They are or suspect they might be pregnant* (Note this warning! "If you are taking this drug to avoid pregnancy the drug company is warning of possible complications to you in addition to terminating the pregnancy." Food for thought ladies!)

• *They have abnormal vaginal bleeding.*

• *They are taking nevirapine, rifampin, or St. John's wort.*

• *They have had a stroke or history of bleeding of the brain, known or suspected breast cancer, or a blood clotting disorder.*

Those with pre-existing medical conditions also are cautioned about levonorgestrel. Those with diabetes, food allergies, or a history of ectopic pregnancy are warned about risks to their health, and a long list of drugs also can interact badly with levonorgestrel.

The last warning about levonorgestrel would be laughable if it wasn't so deadly serious: *Check with your health care provider before you start, stop, or change the dose of any medicine.*

This drug was approved for over-the-counter sales precisely to circumvent the involvement of medical professionals who might actually know and care about their patients. Also keep in mind that your teenage daughter can buy this over the counter, and you wouldn't even know she had taken it unless she experiences complications. Then Mom and Dad, finally understanding what has happened, are left to deal with the physical, emotional, and financial consequences.

The second drug, most commonly known as *ella*, employs ulipristal acetate and can be taken up to five days after unprotected intercourse. Medical associations that are funded by and answer to the U.S. government insist that emergency contraception is not an abortifacient, and the mainstream media regularly repeats this as a fact. The problem is, it's a lie.

Let's go back to Plan B for a second. Here's how the Plan B website describes how levonorgestrel ensures a woman gets her next menstrual period on time:

"Temporarily stops the release of an egg from the ovary, prevents fertilization, prevents a fertilized egg from attaching to the uterus. Plan B is not an abortion pill—if you take plan B, you will not be terminating a pregnancy."

That last sentence is a lie, but you have to be familiar with some history to spot it.

In 1965, five years after the FDA approved the birth control pill, the definition of pregnancy was changed. Instead of considering a woman pregnant once the egg has been fertilized, the new order declared that pregnancy begins with implantation. So if Plan B prevents implantation, no harm, no foul, right? Wrong. If pregnancy begins at fertilization (which it does), even the birth control pill is an abortifacient. That fact alone would greatly cut into sales of the Pill, so the easiest thing to do to ensure maximum profit was to change the definition of pregnancy.

Remember earlier in this chapter when we talked about the zygote? This organism, created when a sperm fertilizes an egg, is "the unique first edition of a new individual complete with a genetic blueprint." Within 24-30 hours, the zygote has completed its first cell division. If that's not life, what is?

Several years after Plan B hit the market, ella was approved, widening the emergency window to five days. This is what the American Association of Pro-Life Obstetricians & Gynecologists wrote in 2010, after the FDA approved ella.

> *"Ella is the first selective progesterone receptor modulator (SPRM) available in the United States for the indication of "emergency contraception (EC)." This class of drug (SPRM) blocks progesterone which is necessary to maintain a pregnancy. It disables the uterine lining, compromising its ability to form a functional "secretory" endometrium—the lining which nourishes the fertilized, implanting, new human baby. This effectively deprives the brand new human child of oxygen and nutrients, and the child dies. This is an abortifacient action.*

> *"Today's approval, labeling 'ella' as emergency contraception, is deceptive and dangerous to women and their newly conceived baby. Women deserve to know that 'ella' can cause death of the embryo, and the FDA is deliberately misleading women by mislabeling 'ella' only as contraception, and not as abortifacient.*

> *"Don't miss this important fact: Ella only delays ovulation if taken in the day or so before ovulation happens, i.e., before the luteal surge which stimulates release of the egg. After ovulation, if the egg is fertilized, 'ella' works as a progesterone-blocking abortifacient. How often would you guess a woman takes this in just the right window (a day or two before ovulation) to delay ovulation? Not often. Taken at other times, it has no effect on ovulation.*

> *"The egg must be fertilized on the day of ovulation. (After 1 day, it resists fertilization), And why does 'ella' work for 5 days after ovulation? Because it is on about the 5th day after ovulation and fertilization that the new baby begins to implant—but can't, because the uterine lining function is disabled by 'ella.' This is an abortifacient action. And this is why 'ella' can be used, as advertised, up to 5 days after intercourse."*

What is our zygote, with its complete genetic blueprint, up to at this point? "At six days after fertilization, the zygote begins to embed itself in the inner wall of the mother's uterus." A woman who has swallowed the lie of ella is now on the way to ending the life of her own child.

It's clear what these early pregnancy drugs do to the baby, but what about the woman or girl who swallows these potent pills? Remember, these drugs are sold over the counter at your neighborhood pharmacy and anyone can purchase them regardless of her age. So parents be warned: Your 13, 14, or 15-year-old daughter who might be hiding her sexual activity from you can have access to these drugs.

Your daughter can't even get a Tylenol in school without your consent, but her local pharmacy will dispense these drugs to her without your knowledge.

Unborn babies who make it through the first week after fertilization will face a new hurdle with RU-486, the so-called abortion pill.

RU-486 was developed in France and was in use in Europe long before the FDA approved it in 2000 for use in the United States. The FDA's original protocols called for RU-486, which is actually the first drug in a two-step regimen, to be administered by a doctor and only up to seven weeks since a woman's last menstrual period. But abortion providers began using the pills up to nine weeks, and through "tele-med" conferencing in use in Iowa and Minnesota and spreading rapidly, doctors can be hundreds of miles away from their patients when the first drug—mifepristone—is ingested. The FDA in 2016 changed its recommendation and approved it for use through the ninth week.

Mifepristone is a progesterone counterfeit that tricks the body by filling the progesterone receptor with a key that will not turn the lock. Without progesterone, the placenta is starved and sloughs off, along with the baby, causing an abortion. The second drug, *misoprostol*, taken 24 to 72 hours later, causes the baby to be expelled from the uterus. A woman who takes *misoprostol* at home, as most do, turns her home into an abortion clinic and has to deal with disposing of her dead child on her own. If this is not a back-alley abortion, it is certainly close.

An at-home abortion is not an easy process. A mother can experience heavy bleeding and extreme cramping as she expels her child, and without a doctor nearby, has to decide for herself if and when she needs medical attention. According to the federal Centers for Disease Control, at least 14 women have died from the abortion pill regimen.

Also, RU-486 can fail, allowing the pregnancy to continue. Mothers then have to make a second choice—surgical abortion, or keep the baby they tried to abort.

But now there is a third choice. Mothers who have taken mifepristone and then realize they have made a mistake can find a doctor near them by going to the web site *AbortionPillReversal.com*. That doctor will flood the mother's system with progesterone that will compete with the mifespristone to fill the progesterone receptor. Abortion pill reversals succeed about 60 percent of the time. The very first one was performed by Priests for Life medical advisor Dr. Matt Harrison in North Carolina and he remains in touch with the mother and her little girl who was saved from abortion. If you read about the reversal procedure in the mainstream media, you will have seen it described as "junk science," but the truth is that hundreds of children have been saved.

After nine weeks, RU-486 is no longer an option. Now a woman who does not want the son or daughter in her womb to live is looking at a first-trimester surgical abortion. Nucleus Medical Media is a company that does diagrams of medical procedures for court cases. Here is the firm's diagram of a first trimester abortion.

Suction and Curettage Abortion of a 9 Week Old Fetus

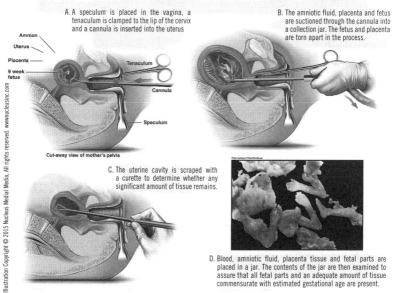

A. A speculum is placed in the vagina, a tenaculum is clamped to the lip of the cervix and a cannula is inserted into the uterus

B. The amniotic fluid, placenta and fetus are suctioned through the cannula into a collection jar. The fetus and placenta are torn apart in the process.

C. The uterine cavity is scraped with a curette to determine whether any significant amount of tissue remains.

D. Blood, amniotic fluid, placenta tissue and fetal parts are placed in a jar. The contents of the jar are then examined to assure that all fetal parts and an adequate amount of tissue commensurate with estimated gestational age are present.

Now let's consider how abortionists describe what happens to the unborn child in a first-trimester abortion.

Dr. Harlan Raymond Giles, in sworn testimony given in U.S. District Court for the Western District of Wisconsin (Madison, WI, May 27, 1999, Case No. 98-C-0305-S), was asked: *"Can the heart of a fetus or embryo still be beating during a suction curettage abortion as the fetus or embryo comes down the cannula?"* His answer: *"For a few seconds to a minute, yes."*

Many people, when asked their position on abortion, say it's OK in the first three months of pregnancy. I wonder if they would have the same response if they realized that the baby's heart is beating during the abortion?

Abortionist Warren Hern, in a textbook he wrote on abortion, said this about first trimester abortion.

> *"The physician will usually first notice a quantity of amniotic fluid, followed by placenta and fetal parts, which may be more or less identifiable."* (*Abortion Practice*, Dr. Warren Hern, p.114, section on First Trimester Abortion).

And here are excerpts from Hern's testimony in a 1999 federal case in Wisconsin.

> *"When we do a suction curettage abortion, you know, roughly one of three things is going to happen during the abortion. One would be that the catheter as it approaches the fetus, you know, tears it and kills it at that instant inside the uterus.*

> *"The second would be that the fetus is small enough and the catheter is large enough that the fetus passes through the catheter and either dies in transit as it's passing through the catheter or dies in the suction bottle after it's actually all the way out."*—Sworn testimony given in U.S. District Court for the Western District of Wisconsin (Madison, WI, May 27, 1999, Case No. 98-C-0305-S).

This is not a blob of tissue, or a clump of cells. This is a baby and it is perfectly legal to kill him, even while his heart is beating!

Second-trimester Abortion

What happens to a baby during a second-trimester abortion? It is even more inhumane, if that's possible. Remember that during the second trimester, moms go through a variety of tests where fetal abnormalities like

Down syndrome, spina bifida and other disorders are diagnosed, and medical professionals can pressure parents to terminate the pregnancy to end the child's life.

Here is the diagram of the second trimester abortion, commonly know as a D & E abortion.

Dilation and Evacuation Abortion of a 23 Week Old Fetus

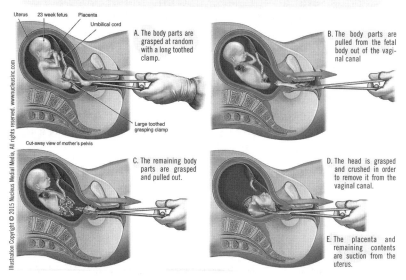

A. The body parts are grasped at random with a long toothed clamp.

B. The body parts are pulled from the fetal body out of the vaginal canal.

C. The remaining body parts are grasped and pulled out.

D. The head is grasped and crushed in order to remove it from the vaginal canal.

E. The placenta and remaining contents are suction from the uterus.

This is how abortionists describe a second-trimester procedure.

"The friction causes the fetus to tear apart. For example, a leg might be ripped off the fetus as it is pulled through the cervix" (U.S.Supreme Court, Gonzales vs. Carhart, April 18, 2007, describing the D&E procedure which is legal).

"We would attack the lower part of the lower extremity first, remove, you know, possibly a foot, then the lower leg at the knee and then finally we get to the hip" (Sworn testimony given in U.S. District Court for the Western District of Wisconsin. Madison, WI, May 27, 1999, Case No. 98-C-0305-S, by Dr. Martin Haskell).

"*Typically the skull is brought out in fragments rather than as a unified piece...*" (Sworn testimony given in U.S. District Court for the Western District of Wisconsin. Madison, WI, May 27, 1999, Case No. 98-C-0305-S, by Dr. Martin Haskell).

"*The procedure changes significantly at 21 weeks because the fetal tissues become much more cohesive and difficult to dismember. This problem is accentuated by the fact that the fetal pelvis may be as much as 5cm in width. The calvaria [head] is no longer the principal problem; it can be collapsed. Other structures, such as the pelvis, present more difficulty. . . .A long curved Mayo scissors may be necessary to decapitate and dismember the fetus. . .*" (From the medical textbook *Abortion Practice*, Dr. Warren Hern, p.154).

"*The doctor grips a fetal part with the forceps and pulls it back through the cervix, . . . continuing to pull even after meeting resistance from the cervix. The friction causes the fetus to tear apart. For example, a leg might be ripped off the fetus as it is pulled through the cervix and out of the woman. The process of evacuating the fetus piece by piece continues until it has been completely removed*" (U.S. Supreme Court, Gonzales vs. Carhart, April 18, 2007, describing the D&E procedure).

"*Let's just say for instance we took a different view, a different tact and we left the leg in the uterus just to dismember it. Well, we'd probably have to dismember it at several different levels because we don't have firm control over it, so we would attack the lower part of the lower extremity first, remove, you know, possibly a foot, then the lower leg at the knee and then finally we get to the hip.*

"*And when the abortion procedure is started we typically know that the fetus is still alive because either we can feel it move as we're making our initial grasps or if we're using some ultrasound visualization when we actually see a heartbeat as we're starting the procedure. It's not unusual at the start of D&E procedures that a limb is acquired first and that that limb is brought through the cervix. . . prior to disarticulation and prior to anything having been done that would have caused the fetal demise up to that point.*

"When you're doing a dismemberment D&E, usually the last part to be removed is the skull itself and it's floating free inside the uterine cavity. . . So it's rather like a ping-pong ball floating around and the surgeon is using his forcep to reach up to try to grasp something that's freely floating around and is quite large relative to the forcep we're using. So typically there's several misdirections, misattempts to grasp.

"Finally at some point either the instruments are managed to be placed around the skull or a nip is made out of some area of the skull that allows it to start to decompress. And then once that happens typically the skull is brought out in fragments rather than as a unified piece. . . " (Sworn testimony given in U.S. District Court for the Western District of Wisconsin. Madison, WI, May 27, 1999, Case No. 98-C-0305-S, by Dr. Martin Haskell).

In plain English, the unborn child is torn apart and brought out through the cervix piece by piece and the abortionist or his assistant must literally count the body parts to make sure they got all of them. If any of the baby's parts are left inside his mother, that can lead to infections or other complications for her.

As horrifying as the second-trimester descriptions were, it gets worse. Abortion is legal in the United States through the seventh, eighth, and even ninth month of pregnancy. Children in the womb who are way past viability have absolutely no protection under the law.

You might remember having heard about a late-term procedure called partial-birth abortion, which was debated in Congress for over a decade before President George W. Bush signed a law banning the barbaric procedure.

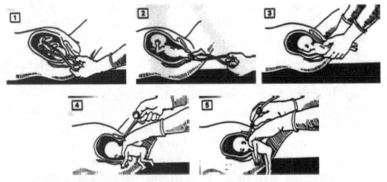

1. Guided by ultrasound, the abortionist grabs the baby's leg with forceps.
2. The baby's leg is pulled out into the birth canal.
3. The abortionist delivers the baby's entire body, except for the head.
4. The abortionist jams scissors into the baby's skull. The scissors are then opened to enlarge the hole.
5. The scissors are removed and a suction catheter is inserted. The child's brains are sucked out, causing the skull to collapse. The dead baby is then removed.

The ban was a good thing for two reasons: It made this terrible procedure illegal and it moved public opinion, as many who would label themselves pro-choice began to see the truth about what legal abortion really entails.

Sadly, the partial-birth abortion ban did not end late-term abortion in the U.S. Many states have enacted laws to prohibit abortion after 20 weeks, and a federal ban is still in the hands of the U.S. Senate. But because these state bans are being challenged in courts and the fate of the federal ban remains to be seen, late-term abortion is still a legal option for all pregnant women.

Without being able to use the partial-birth procedure, abortionists began to rely on a few other techniques. For third-trimester abortions, abortionists load a long needle with the drug digoxin and, guided by ultrasound, inject it through the woman's abdomen and into the baby's heart. This kills the baby. The abortionist then puts something called laminaria into the woman's cervix to begin dilation. In two to three days, the cervix is opened enough to deliver her dead baby. This procedure represents a great risk to the mother.

Why Women Abort

This unborn child has been killed by abortion all because of fears and unfortunate circumstances. Here is a partial list of why women abort their children.

1. The mother would be kicked out of her home if she is too young to have a baby.

2. The mother would be kicked out of school or lose her scholarship.

3. The mother would lose her job or sacrifice a promotion.

4. The father of the baby would abandon her and leave her to raise the baby herself.

5. The mother feels she is not ready to be a mother.

6. The mother and father feel they can't afford to have a baby.

7. Family and friends are pressuring the mother to abort.

8. The baby will be born with a handicap like Down Syndrome or spina bifida.

9. The baby has a fetal anomaly and most likely will die anyway.

10. The mother has cancer or another disease and is told she must choose between her life and that of her baby. (Here we should note that doctors in these cases have two patients—mom and baby—to care for, and no medical condition requires killing one to save the other!)

11. The most important and common reason is that the mother was abused or neglected as a child. In his research, Dr. Ney found that women who had been sexually abused as children can experience deep conflicts about sex that are intensified when they become pregnant. This conflict and anger may result in hostility toward their unborn child. Women who are neglected as children, Dr. Ney found, have a tendency "to select and then coach their partners into being the type of person who neglected or abandoned them as children. Having been abandoned as a child, the threat of being abandoned by a partner who states, 'Get rid of it or I am leaving' is much too threatening." (See: Ney PG. Psychiatric and Demographic Factors that Determine Pregnancy Outcome WebmedCentral 2013 4(1) SM c003978).

Remember the beginning of the chapter when you met the unborn child in all his wonder? What's the difference between the child going through extraordinary transformation on its journey to birth and the child sucked from the womb, or dismembered, or killed by a shot to the heart? It is all about circumstance. Wanted babies are the guests of honor at showers and gender reveal parties. Unwanted babies lose their lives at filthy, unregulated abortion clinics at the hands of doctors who long ago violated their Hippocratic Oath.

The death of every baby killed by abortion represents the epicenter of a trauma that extends out from the mother to a wider circle of victims.

Chapter Four

Always a Mom!

A woman is a mother from the moment of conception and an abortion doesn't erase that fact. Abortion does not turn back the clock. Abortion is not a giant eraser that rids everyone involved of the problem. In this chapter I will show, through personal testimonies and examples of medical complications, how abortion impacts the mother.

First let's take a brief look at a contraceptive that is supposed to prevent pregnancy.

Depo-Provera is a long-acting birth control method for women. It is made up of a hormone similar to progesterone and is given as an injection by a doctor into the woman's arm or buttocks. Each shot provides protection against pregnancy for up to 12 to 14 weeks, but the shot must be received once every 12 weeks to provide full protection. Birth control with Depo-Provera begins immediately after the first shot given within the first five days of a woman's menstrual period. The manufacturer recommends that it be used with caution by adolescents.

Depo-Provera can cause a number of side effects, including: Irregular menstrual periods, or no periods at all, headaches, nervousness, depression, dizziness, changes in appetite, weight gain, excessive growth of facial and body hair, and loss of bone mineral density. More serious side effects include an increased risk of HIV infection, breast and cervical cancer, blood clots, ectopic pregnancy, reduced fertility, and excessive weight gain.

Prolonged use of Depo-Provera may result in loss of significant bone mineral density, increasing the risk of osteoporosis. This risk is more likely for those who have been taking it for longer than two years, particularly when other risk factors exist, such as family history and chronic alcohol and/or tobacco use. All women on Depo-Provera are advised to get adequate calcium and Vitamin D (through diet and/or supplements) to help prevent osteoporosis. To some—especially young, sexually active girls—Depo Provera may sound like a foolproof method of preventing pregnancy, but this is not a benign drug. Here's one woman's experience and believe me, hers is not an isolated case.

Kimmy from California had this to say:

> *"I got pregnant while on Depo-Provera. Planned Parenthood said I was eleven weeks pregnant but should abort the pregnancy as the Depo could cause my baby to have severe brain damage, deformed limbs, etc. Years later I found the most drastic problem my baby would've faced was a premature birth. I am devastated to learn I could have kept my baby if I hadn't been misinformed. Instead I lost my baby, had three D&Cs, a year-and-a-half of constant irregular bleeding, and have a lifetime of regret."*

Failed contraception leads to abortion because that is exactly what the abortion clinics are selling women. If you are not ready to be a mom, they tell you, we can fix that for you.

Earlier in chapter three we talked about Plan B and ella, the so-called emergency contraception methods that can and often do work as abortifacients. But what do these drugs do to the mother of this unwanted child?

If the mother has had a stroke or family history of strokes, or bleeding on the brain, known or suspected breast cancer, or a blood clotting disorder she should not take morning-after, or week-after pills. These warnings come from the drug manufacturer but because these medications can be purchased at pharmacies without a prescription—and yes even your teenage daughter can have access to these pills—many people overlook the safety warnings. Think about it, when was the last time you read all the pamphlets that came with your prescriptions?

RU-486

At-home pregnancy tests can now detect pregnancies very early, which has led to a surge in the use of the abortion pill. One-quarter of abortions are now performed this way.

The abortion pill regimen, also called RU-486, uses two deadly compounds. The first is mifepristone, a synthetic steroid that works by blocking the effects of progesterone, the natural hormone required to maintain the lining of the uterus during pregnancy. Mifepristone starves the womb of progesterone, the lining of the womb breaks down, and the developing embryo is starved. Twenty-four to 48 hours later, the woman takes the second medication—misoprostol—at home. This medication causes the uterus to contract, expelling the dead baby.

The woman is the one actually causing the death of her unborn child and her bathroom and bedroom become the abortion clinic. This is even more traumatizing than a surgical abortion because of the fact that the mother is actually performing the abortion on herself.

Let's take a look at a few of these cases in the words of the women themselves. These are just a few of the many testimonies on the website *www.SilentNoMore.com.*

Patricia from Georgia writes:

"I had just started a new job and my sister was due soon in her pregnancy. All was great; I had

a new job, my ex-boyfriend-to-be and I were in a good place, and I had a nephew on the way.

"*A few days later my nephew was born, and I found out I was pregnant. I told my boyfriend about it, and he said he would be supportive in whatever I decided, no matter what I chose. So I started thinking that I didn't want to take the spotlight away from my sister and her newborn son. I did not want to risk losing my job by doing horribly at work because of my crazy morning sickness, which lasted almost my whole work day. I didn't want to put my college classes at risk. I didn't want to bring a baby into a complicated relationship. I was just scared, completely scared, and I had no idea what I should do. After talking with the father of my child, I decided that I would get an abortion. We thought it would be the best thing for us.*

"*At 8.3 weeks, I took the abortion pill at a nearby clinic. I didn't think much else of it, until it was time to take the next four pills the following day. That's when the excruciating pain began. There were unbearable cramps, and something that felt as if they were contractions. That went on for hours until I felt a large lump leave me. Seconds later, I cried. I cried and couldn't stop. I instantly regretted what I had just done, but I decided to put on a brave face because I 'did the right thing for me.'*

"*From then on, things seemed okay. I thought it was over. I continued on with life blindly, not realizing who I had become and what I had lost. Three months later I was single again. What I didn't see was that I had lost myself and a part of me had died. I became numb, easily annoyed and angered, distant, and I goofed off. I stopped caring about how my relationships were going, and I did not want to be intimate in any way. I became obsessed with money and this future I was preparing for. At* the time, I couldn't see why, but now I do. I tried so hard to never think about it without seeing the real problem. My abortion was the problem. I would have been 22 weeks now and my baby would have been born in October. Maybe my mother's prediction that the baby was a girl would have been right. My nephew would be having a cousin soon. But all of this was gone and would not come true.

"I should have never had the abortion. I never thought things would be this way. If I had known, or at least have been warned that that 'little decision' would have this effect on me, I would have never followed through with it. Had I just held on a little longer and thought things through, I would have chosen to keep her. If there was anything I could do to take it back, I wouldn't even think twice. I'd do whatever it takes. I would be feeling her kicks right now and I would be talking to her and wishing I could see her already. I would be having my baby girl in my arms soon."

Abortion advocates always warn that restricting abortion will lead women back to dangerous do-it-yourself abortions, but with RU-486, we have already arrived there. This is not health care. There is no compassion for the mother and the shockwaves from this at-home abortion are no less profound.

Solome from New York wrote this about her RU-486 abortion:

"I made an appointment and went to the clinic. They said I could take the pill because I found out in the early stages. A part of me thought that as long as they didn't go in there with any metal tools and suck it out, it would be different and less gruesome. Boy, was I wrong! The time between my visit and my appointment went by really fast. I was numb and completely disconnected from everything around me. I would start crying as soon as

I left work until I fell asleep at 4 or 5 a.m. I would walk down the street crying, or in the train, or when I saw babies and pregnant women.

"I went to the clinic on a Thursday afternoon and took my first pill. I was given prescription pills for the next day. It took about 30 minutes for the cramps and bleeding to start. I remember thinking, 'OK, so this should be over in an hour or so.' But it wasn't. During that time I felt like my inside was being torn and sliced to pieces. I had blood all over my legs and went in the tub to wash them. The cramps got so bad I couldn't even move. I couldn't even cry. It was worse than anything I've ever seen on TV. All the labor and contractions they show were nothing compared to this. I couldn't get to my phone to dial 911 and go to the emergency room. I lay there for hours thinking, 'I deserve this; I brought this on myself.' Right before the fetus came out, I started vomiting everything I had in my system since that morning. Then I bled some more and hurt some more. I started praying curled up in blood in the tub, for the first time in years. I don't remember the last time I prayed before this happened. After hours of hurting, I finally felt a huge physical relief, and the pain was immediately gone. I managed to get up. When I turned around I saw the most heartbreaking thing I've ever seen my entire life. I saw my child. It was at that moment that it finally sunk in properly. I really had been pregnant. I had been carrying the life I created inside of me until that very moment.

"Right after that, I cried and cried for hours. I put my child in a little box and kept saying I was sorry for what I had done. I was weeping and screaming, but nothing could turn back time. I felt like a part of me died. I felt angry. I felt guilty. I felt like my world was coming to an end and that I was the most terrible person on this earth. I couldn't *believe what I was looking at. It was the most beautiful thing I ever created, and I destroyed it.*

"For the next few weeks, my eating habits changed. I lost some weight, and I got weak. It was hard to keep up because I was a trainer, and I had to keep coming up with all sorts of excuses as to why I wasn't working out and so forth. I couldn't keep up with the long hours and staying in an environment where people were so concerned about how they looked and their health. I couldn't care less what I looked like or how much I weighed or if I could lift or whatever. My relationship with my boyfriend had terrible ups and downs. It seemed like he recovered much quicker than I had. After all, he was far away and didn't have to see any of what I went through. I felt tired and useless. I spent days just crying, staying in bed, and living in a disorganized, messy room."

I don't understand how anyone can read Solome's words—"I saw my child"—and continue to insist that RU-486 abortion is good healthcare for women.

This is how Yanette in Virginia describes her RU-486 abortion:

"I had an abortion because I got pregnant by this guy I didn't even like while I was taking a semester off from college. I decided that it would be much easier to have an abortion than to have a baby. I thought I wouldn't be able to finish school and I would be the embarrassment of my family. I had always been a 'goodie two shoes,' so worried about what others thought of me. I couldn't imagine telling my family that I was pregnant; I thought they would be so ashamed of me. So, after thinking about it for a few days, I decided that I was going to be selfish and live my life for me.

"I still remember the day. I was living in Maryland and I drove down to Baltimore by myself. I went to

a 'women's health clinic,' checked myself in, and waited for them to call my name. I went to speak with a counselor, who asked me if I was sure I wanted to do this. I told her yes. Then she asked me if I had come by myself and if I had anybody there with me. I broke down in tears. I had no one. After waiting for me to get myself together she took me to pay my bill, and of course my insurance paid for it. They took me to a room and gave me two pills in my hand. The doctor told me that the pills would induce a miscarriage and that once I started taking them I could not stop. I took one in the office and the other I could take at home, a few hours from then. After taking the first pill they released me.

"I came out and it was like nothing had happened. By the time I got home, waited, read my instructions, waited, and read the instructions a few more times, enough time had passed for me to take the next pill. I took it and went to sleep. I woke up in excruciating pain; it was like cramps, but the worst feeling I had ever had. I laid there for a moment, so thrown off by the pain that I forgot what was even going on. When I remembered what I had done, I ran to the bathroom and stayed there for the next three hours while I miscarried. I sat there, crying and in pain, passing my baby, trying not to make too much noise because I didn't want my aunt to get suspicious. Once it was all over I wanted to die. Blood and tissue were everywhere. I looked in the toilet and all I could think is 'those are pieces of my baby.'

"I did make it back to college, but I was haunted by everything I had done in Maryland. I struggled to overcome the grief, shame, and condemnation I felt for years. I felt I could not trust anybody and I did not believe that anyone could really love me, especially if they knew what I had done. So I didn't talk about it. My emotions were all over the place. One minute I was happy, the next I was angry and

*then I would be a sobbing puddle of tears. And no
one really knew why.*

*"I went even more inside of myself because I felt
like no one understood me. If they only knew what
I struggled with every day they would understand.
But if I told them the truth, I wouldn't be able to
live inside the lie I created for myself. For a time,
I would rather have them think I was crazy than
know that I was a murderer. I became even more of
an alcoholic, I smoked weed more than I had ever
before. I did all sorts of stupid things with stupid
people. There is a pain so deep, so profound, that
comes from losing a child—a pain that only inten-
sifies when it is by your own hands."*

As you can see by these few examples, women who
use RU-486 to abort their children face a unique pain
and trauma because they have to try to live in the very
place where their innocent child died.

Surgical Abortion

When a mother is beyond nine weeks in the baby's
gestation, a surgical abortion is performed to terminate
the pregnancy. The first procedure is called a vacuum
aspiration and it is used from the ninth through twelfth
week, and sometimes later. Let's consider what mothers
themselves have to say about this type of abortion:

Nicole Peck, a regional coordinator from Connecticut
shares:

*"I had an abortion at the age of 15 out of fear and
shame. Unfortunately, the real truth about abortion was never given to me. The abortion facility
never performed a pregnancy test or explained the
procedure to me. I was never told about the risks
of abortion such as death, breast cancer, endome-
triosis, and infertility. I don't know if a doctor performed the abortion or if a nurse helped him. There*

was no counseling or compassion from the staff. No one held my hand during or after the abortion.

"What I remember most vividly is the sucking sound of the machine during the abortion and feeling like my insides would be ripped out. They provided juice, cookies, and antibiotics after the abortion. The staff did their jobs and took my money and that was it!

"That's the LIE! It was not IT! I felt like I had no other choice—my dreams of college and a career would be gone with a baby. Deep down I don't think I really wanted the abortion, but could see no other way out. I was scared and felt alone in my relationship with my boyfriend!

"Immediately after the abortion, I felt relief. I could move on now, or so I thought. Emotionally, I was distant and empty after the abortion and contemplated suicide. On the outside everything looked good, but I had a huge hole in my heart that could not be healed. My relationship with the father ended when we graduated from high school and we didn't tell our parents at the time.

"Abortion was supposed to help me and it didn't. It created many years of anguish, lies, and heartache because I refused to face it and I could not forgive myself. I was NEVER able to conceive a child after my abortion because of the physical damage it caused. The truth is abortion scars women."

Nicole thought the abortion would solve her immediate problems as a high school student afraid to have a baby, afraid to tell her parents. Her abortion haunted her and years later when she did marry and wanted to have a baby, she couldn't. The physical damage from her abortion left her unable to conceive a child. Nicole did find healing through an abortion recovery program called Rachel's Vineyard and she and her husband later adopted two beautiful baby boys. But remember, their own family genealogy was cut short by that abortion. The shockwave impacted her whole family.

Angelina Steenstra, the Silent No More national coordinator in Canada whom we met earlier, had her abortion in upstate New York and had this to say:

"I had an abortion to erase the result of a date rape.

"My world felt unreal until the icy cold instruments entered my body. I felt severe physical pain. Told to be still, I was assured it wouldn't take long. Next, I heard the sound of a high-pitched machine that sucked out the contents of my womb. As I saw the bottle next to my right foot fill up with blood, I wondered, 'Is there a baby? Is there a soul? Who sees what I'm doing?'

"There was a moment when I experienced a sense of death and the reality of a soul. I cried from the depths of my being. There was no turning back—no reversing the contents of the bottle. Deep inside I knew that what was happening was wrong. Something was broken, and I could not fix it. This realization was devastating, I wanted to die.

"Immediately after the abortion, I was sedated. I hoped I would never wake up. Told to leave the abortion facility, I boarded a bus. As I saw myself in the window, I remember thinking, 'I hate you. You will never be able to fix this!' Self-hatred took hold of me.

"As time went on, I tried to start over to get away from the guilt, shame, and depression. I changed my name, address, job, and friends. I lived in a secretive prison of self-hatred and condemnation. Turning to alcohol, drugs, and sexual affairs to numb the pain, I fell away from friends and family and became suicidal.

"In desperation, I found a counselor who validated all my feelings and called my past actions what

they were, sinful. The truth gave me so much relief that I thought the abortion was behind me.

"*I married. Abortion again took front and center. Pregnancy, babies, doctors, being a mother became abortion connectors. To eradicate the fears, I poured myself into my job. In self-loathing, I starved myself and smoked profusely. With every puff and drink of alcohol, I swallowed the painful memories of the abortion. Sounds of vacuum cleaners and dentist drills sent me into emotional anguish. I couldn't conceive and thought God was punishing me.*

"*Healing began with an ectopic pregnancy, which took the life of our son. Grieving his loss, I found courage to face the abortion. The image of an aborted baby unbottled my tears.*

"*My first pregnancy was a person, Sarah Elizabeth. I would grieve her loss, ask forgiveness from her, from God, and from others, with the help of retreats, such as Rachel's Vineyard and Entering Canaan, and a weekly post-abortion support group.*

"*When I hit the 40th anniversary of Sarah's death, I discovered once again that healing is an ongoing journey. Nothing prepared me for the gut-wrenching grief triggered by family weddings at this point in our life cycle. Losing Sarah and her brother, Joseph Michael, our genealogy, and our family life is agonizing.*

"*Abortion did not undo the date rape or the positive pregnancy test. Abortion eliminated my child and robbed me of future children.*"

Notice in Angelina's case that the abortion did not heal her of the date rape. In fact, she got over the rape, but the abortion caused her lasting physical and psychological pain and damage. The abortion didn't erase the trauma of the rape; it traumatized her all over again.

Later when she married and wanted children, she suffered an ectopic pregnancy. She never conceived again. The shockwaves of that abortion loss impacted her husband, her parents and siblings, and Angelina most of all.

Lynn from California writes:

"I had an abortion because I wanted to hide the shame of engaging in pre-marital sex. My boyfriend and I were supposed to be Christians and our families would have been embarrassed. Even though he was working full-time and could have supported us, he didn't offer to marry me. We were already making plans to get married and had bought property for our first home. My parents made it clear that I was on my own and not to expect any help from them in raising the baby. My father never confronted my boyfriend and we never told his parents. I think if I had told his parents, they would have supported my having the baby. I couldn't think clearly because of the panic of the situation. Later, I thought that I should have left my parents and boyfriend to live with my grandma and have the baby.

"During the abortion, I was frightened, disgusted, and deeply miserable. I felt silent protests inside of me. But, once you've signed the paperwork and are in the clinic, you will not be coming out pregnant. I was even willing to let them just keep the money. Yet, I remained silent. It felt like rape. I remember them giving all the women Valium and looking around the room at all the other women and girls and thinking we were like lambs to the slaughter.

"Immediately after the abortion I felt despondent and wanted to die. Other women in the recovery room were sobbing and equally miserable. I didn't want to have anything to do with my boyfriend anymore and I know his failure to protect

me and the baby led to the demise of our later marriage. I had him take me home, but no one was there. Then, I had him take me to my parents at my brother's baseball game because I didn't want to be alone.

"As time went on after the abortion I felt numb and hardened. It seems that my heart was deeply scarred at the same time my uterus was. There was nothing soft left in me. The essence of my femininity was destroyed. I became driven to succeed and any sweetness in my nature I previously possessed was gone. I was not able to have intimacy with people because I couldn't really trust them, certainly not Christians. I was very successful professionally, but my marriage to the baby's father ended with my adultery and I became sexually promiscuous. I adopted a jaded attitude towards men—I can't really depend upon them or rely upon them for any support. My life began unraveling about twenty years after the abortion. The more successful I became professionally, the more I disdained that 'successful' life and resented that I didn't have a family. When I found out that the abortion 20 years earlier had left me sterile, I fell apart. All the hurt and rage began boiling inside me. I resented my ex-husband and his family. He was able to move on and have children with his second wife."

In Lynn's case you see how she really didn't want that abortion, but she wasn't given the emotional support she needed from the father of the baby, and fear of what family and friends would think of her out-of-wedlock pregnancy contributed to her decision. She stuffed the trauma and her feelings way deep down but it surfaced later, destroying her marriage. Because of the physical damage done during the abortion, she was never able to conceive a child when she wanted a family. That abortion shockwave also took away her parent's grandchild and any future grandchildren.

Kelly from Georgia recalls her two abortions:

"I had two abortions over a decade ago because I was already a divorced single mom and didn't want my Christian parents to know I was sleeping with my boyfriend. I remember every sight, sound, and smell in the clinic. I felt like a number—rushed in and out and treated with indifference. I suffered for months after the second abortion until doctors discovered I had an incomplete abortion and there were still parts of my child inside of me.

"Immediately after the abortion I felt a mixture of sadness and anger and vowed never to share what I had done with anyone. As time went on, I medicated my feelings with food and alcohol, and I suffered with paralyzing guilt, shame, and depression. I found help and forgiveness through attending the Surrendering the Secret Bible study and through blogging, singing, and speaking about my experiences.

"Recently, I found out that the doctor who did my abortions has had his license suspended for the fourth time because of the complications women like myself had after being in his clinic and because he was doing abortions into the third trimester. This has only fueled my longing to stand up for our children and be a loud voice that says ABORTION HURTS WOMEN."

You might think Kelly's experience of an incomplete abortion is rare but sadly it happens more often than you might think. As I discussed in my previous book, *Recall Abortion,* I was once in an emergency room in a major hospital in New Jersey and the woman in the next cubicle was hemorrhaging from complications from an abortion that was performed that morning at a nearby abortion clinic. Parts of her baby were left inside and she was being rushed into surgery for what could have included a hysterectomy. But later she was told she was one of the "lucky ones," who wasn't permanently damaged by her abortion.

Medical complications create other long-term problems, such as infertility. When Jewish families look at their family portraits, it is always with the understanding that many are missing because of the Holocaust—not just the people killed by the Nazis, but the generations that would have succeeded them. Abortion shockwaves have impacted our families the same way.

Crystal from Kentucky shared:

"I was still the fun party girl in college until my drinking and promiscuous behavior finally caught up with me. I was eighteen and pregnant. When I got up enough courage to tell the father, all he said was that he would take care of everything. He was 22 years old and in his fifth and final year of engineering school. Before I knew what hit me, he was driving me to the abortion clinic. I was never asked what I wanted to do about the baby, he decided for me. I only remember being terrified, mad, and shocked all at the same time. I did not say a single word to him in the car on the way to the abortion clinic. He had borrowed money from his fraternity to pay for the abortion.

"When we got there, the first thing they wanted was payment in full. This was back in 2000, and then it was $600 for a second-trimester abortion and an additional $600 for anesthesia. Anesthesia was not required until the third trimester. Well, we were both college students and broke. So I was thirteen weeks pregnant and did not have the option for any anesthesia. After paying at the counter, we sat in the waiting room, for what felt like hours. All the women sat scared and silent. He was silent also, not knowing what, if anything, he should say to me.

"Next it was time for the ultrasound to verify gestational age. I had to beg and plead to see the

monitor screen, which they refused to let me see until I argued with them for over fifteen minutes. Finally, they turned the screen toward me. I could see my BABY, not a ball of tissue or clump of cells, but my BABY moving around. Face, hands, and even the heart beating. I got to see the tiny child turning somersaults in my belly. After this I expressed my second thoughts to the father. He replied with, 'Honey, I love you, and when we both graduate engineering school, we can be together like I want. Then if you want to have a baby we can.' He told me whatever he had to in order to make sure that I had that abortion and got rid of the problem before anyone found out.

"A woman called me back again. This time I was brought to a small room. No counseling or education was done. I was only given one-sided opinions, no medical facts. I was lied to! I was told that there were rarely any side effects. 'Most women go out that night,' I was told. It's really no big deal. It will all be over soon. All other medical procedures require INFORMED consent, but I guess abortion clinics don't have to follow those guidelines, because that would probably significantly reduce their profits!

"After filling my head with lies, they took me to a cold room for the procedure. It was filled with a doctor and many women dressed like nurses, but who knows what their credentials were. The first time I met the doctor, he was putting my feet in stirrups. As I lay back on the bed, I started sternly saying no several times. That's when the doctor had the nurses hold me down. He clamped the tenaculum on. That is a metal device with huge pointed teeth that go into a woman's cervix to pull it down and open. When that clamped on, I yelled, 'STOP! I can't do this!' That is when the doctor told me, 'Don't scream, you'll scare the other patients.' I felt violated and threatened, both physically and *emotionally. Keep in mind, with me being thirteen weeks pregnant, they did a D & C on me without any anesthesia! It felt like they were cutting and scraping my insides out. All I could hear was a loud, continuous sucking noise. This excruciating pain lasted several minutes. I was drenched in sweat. After they killed my baby, they told me to get dressed, (which I almost passed out doing), and took me to a room in the back for about an hour. There were several women in that room with the same empty looks on their faces. I sat there in shock and disbelief of what I had just done. When I returned to the waiting room to meet Gregg, he never said a word about what he had just made me do. I felt like my life had ended with my baby's life on November 13, 2000. Self-punishment, guilt, and self-condemnation ate away at me, alienated me from God, inhibited any healthy relationships, destroyed my self-esteem, and paralyzed my personal growth.*

"I stopped eating, drank all night every night to numb the pain and fill that empty void. Abortion took my soul, and now I didn't deserve happiness. I felt unlovable. I hated myself, and I was unworthy of forgiveness. I deserved to be punished for what I did. I murdered my baby! For years, I couldn't even get a pap smear without passing out, because I would have physical flashbacks. During a pap smear, my body was actually feeling the physical pain of my abortion all over again. I felt I deserved jail time for murder, or even worse: eternal hell, which was exactly what I gave myself. A part of me died each time (with the abuse and abortion) until there was nothing left. So I dropped out of engineering school, moved back home at eighteen years old and 82 pounds, and got back with an ex-boyfriend. I punished myself by marrying him, because I felt that was what I deserved. My self-punishment lasted over six years.

"When I attended a Rachel's Vineyard retreat, I found much healing and repentance. I got back my spirit and found purpose in my life. I was able to heal and get closure with my abortion.

"I have been through it all: cervical dysplagia, pre-cervical cancer, LEEP procedure, multiple colposcopies (biopsies), surgeries to remove uterine scar tissue, pelvic inflammatory disease (PID), and other gynecological problems.

"I have lost years of my life, and I'm still paying for it to this day. Another lifelong effect of abortion I'm still struggling with is children. I avoid babies, pregnant women, and families every chance I get. Do I deserve kids? Could I be a good parent? Would a child cause resentment? Could I bond with another child? Could I have a healthy relationship with a child? Would I be good enough? I don't feel I deserve to be a mother, so I remain thirty years old and childless. Not a day goes by that I don't think of my unborn daughter.

"Some ask, 'Why relive your painful past? Why not forget and move on?' Those people are asking the impossible! The questions should be: 'Why would one continue to endure the burden of suffering post-abortion pain in shamed silence?'"

Nancy Tanner from Virginia writes:

"I already had two little girls and had just started dating the man who would become my second husband. When I told him I was pregnant, I was expecting him to say we would make it work. But he said it was my choice and he would pay for the abortion.

"I saw my regular ob/gyn at Kaiser and she referred me to Planned Parenthood. Kaiser even made the appointment for me and arranged for my insurance to cover it.

"I was a teacher and I had the day off for a Jewish holiday the day I went to a Planned Parenthood in Washington, D.C. Outside there was a pro-life woman who handed me a rose. That was the only love I saw all day. But the first thing they did at Planned Parenthood was take my rose away. They said they would hold it for me.

"As I was filling out paperwork, I saw a permission slip that dealt with disposal of the 'products of conception.' It said Planned Parenthood could dispose of the tissue as they wished. I said I didn't want to sign it, and they said I had to or I couldn't have the abortion. I didn't want my baby to be used for scientific research and I was told 'don't worry, it's not a baby.' I told her I had two daughters already and I knew what a baby was. What she said next was very revealing, but I didn't realize it at that time. She said, 'We don't think it's a baby.'

"I had changed my mind and I was looking for a way out of going through with the abortion so I thought about not signing the consent form. But the Planned Parenthood staffer told me that 'what you think of as a baby will be used for something good.' She asked me if I was an organ donor and I replied I was. She said this was a similar value and that I should give honor to what I thought was my child by signing it. I signed the form.

"The room where they killed my child was cold and dirty. I was on the table but wanted to leave and I was pushed back down and they said that it was too late to change my mind. They said it would be quick and painless and I would be fine.

"When the doctor came in, he said nothing to me, he just jammed this thing inside me saying, 'You will feel a little pressure.' I heard the horrible sound of the machine that would suck my baby from my womb. I can still hear it. I hear it now. The cramping was horrific. I felt as if my insides were

*being torn out. I cried and the nurse said I should
take her hand and squeeze it. She pushed me down
on the table when I tried to sit up.*

"Right next to me, at eye level, was a jar connected to the vacuum and I saw it fill up with fluid
and blood. It was the remains of my baby. I wanted
to die.

"After that machine was finally turned off, the
doctor took the jar and right in front of me, he
dumped the contents onto a tray and started looking for the pieces of my baby. 'I can't find all the
parts,' he said, 'How pregnant were you?' He yelled
at me! 'If you get an infection it's not my fault.'
Then he turned the machine on and vacuumed
some more. That was worse than the first time.

"The doctor left and told a woman to look for the
parts. I was crying and wanted to use my tears to
baptize my baby. The woman told me not to worry.
'I baptize all the babies' she said. It gave me comfort to think that she would do that, but I thought
how bizarre that someone involved in the death of
my child would care about his soul.

"In the recovery room, we were laid out on
canvas cots. Most of the women were crying and
wouldn't look at each other but the one next to me
told me she had just had her sixth abortion. She
said she never intended to get pregnant, but when-
ever she did, she would just make an appointment.
She advised me that when I left, I should bury the
memory deep and it would never bother me, until
the next time I had an abortion. I knew then I
would never be back.

"When I left, I stopped at the desk and asked for
my tissue donation consent form back because I
wanted to rip it up. They told me 'it's too late, we
don't have it anymore.' I asked for my rose back
and was told they had thrown it away because it

was upsetting the other women. They told me to call my doctor if I ran a high fever.

"The pro-lifer with the roses was gone when I left.

"My abortion wasn't quick and it wasn't pain-less and I wasn't fine. I'm still not fine. I have been through healing and I am very active in pro-life now, but it has been very hard to watch the Planned Parenthood videos that exposed the fact that they are selling aborted baby body parts and profiting from it. I want to look away but I won't let myself. I see that baby whose remains were poured into a dish and I remember that's what my baby looked like."

You can see that Nancy really didn't want her abortion. The man she was about to marry basically told her to have the abortion. Even at the clinic she was looking for a way out. The horrific time in the clinic has left an indelible mark on Nancy. Yes, she has come back to the Church and her faith. She has also attended an abortion recovery program, Rachel's Vineyard, and is involved as a regional coordinator with the Silent No More Awareness Campaign. She is in a better place psychologically, emotionally, and spiritually, and yet she will never forget that day in the Planned Parenthood abortion clinic.

Now let's take a look at what happens to women who have abortions late in the pregnancy. Remember, abortion is legal through all nine months of pregnancy. Again, this is touted as healthcare for women, when there is nothing healthy about it.

Charlene from Arizona shared:

"I had an abortion because I was told my son was sick at his 20-week ultrasound. I was told that he had what amounted to an inoperable problem with his brain. I was scared. I had seen my only

cousin (the only other child in my family) live a life of torment because of brain damage he suffered in utero. I thought it would be kind to spare my child that suffering. I thought no one would love him or care about him. I also, selfishly, worried that my husband (who had been difficult to convince regarding children) would refuse to have any more children if we had an unhealthy child to care for in our family. I was afraid of the expense. I was uncertain that insurance would cover a child born with a health condition. I was afraid he wouldn't be able to get the care he needed because we didn't have tons of money to throw at his problem. I was out of my mind with fear.

"I was told by family members to think of my 'living children' or that 'it wasn't the end of the world.' I was told that keeping my sick son would be selfish on my part.

"We had to travel out of state and stay with relatives. The procedure took two days to complete. First, they stuck a needle in my belly to stop my son's heart, then they stuck rods in me to forcefully dilate the cervix. I spent that night in extreme pain, but the psychological pain was even greater than the physical pain. Because I knew my son was dead inside me and I had killed him. I knew I was carrying his corpse.

"People said to me that this was no big deal. They said women lose babies all the time and carry them, dead, without even knowing it. But, I knew and this was different.

"The next morning, we went to a mortuary. We made arrangements for our son to be cremated. This wasn't technically necessary (I'd been told), but I wanted his remains treated with respect.

"I sat there in the office of the mortician, with my dead baby in my belly. We were out of state, so *they would have to mail him to us. We picked out a container for his remains. I felt like I was slowly losing my mind. The mortician spoke of God's will. This wasn't God. This was the devil and I was in hell.*

"I doubt his remains were treated well, even though we did this. My husband went with me to the clinic. We sat in a waiting room filled with teenagers and other young women there for early abortions. Most were there with other women. I was visibly pregnant and there with my husband. I felt angry that there were so many women and their babies were all probably healthy—but condemned to die anyway. Why? But, what made my abortion so much more 'moral'? Who were we—teenage or otherwise—to say who has the right to be born and who doesn't?

"They moved us to another waiting room for the late-term abortions. Another woman was there with her husband. We didn't speak. She was also visibly pregnant. They gave me something to put in my mouth to start contractions. The pain was unbearable. I had been through natural childbirth twice by this time. The pain was worse. It was an unnatural pain. It was hell.

"Eventually, they gave me anesthesia and I was unconscious until I woke up in the recovery room in pain again. My stomach was flattened. I was dizzy and disoriented. My husband was waiting for me in another room. I asked to see my baby to say good-bye. They told me this would be too horrific, but the doctor gave me foot- and hand-prints. I told the doctor this was how it had to be and thanked him. But deep down I knew I was wrong, and I missed my son, and I hated myself.

"I hated myself the more I looked at the prints. They were so tiny. He had been so precious. Even more so, because he was sick. He was sick and he needed my help and I threw him away. I didn't save him from suffering. I prevented him from living.

"I sought out others who were grieving late-term abortion for poor prenatal diagnosis. We came up with excuses for each other. We said 98 percent of people who get this diagnosis do what we did. As if murder became moral by consensus. We were right to save our children from suffering, we told each other and ourselves. Ours were moral abortions because we weren't slutty, irresponsible teenagers.

"And we were wrong. I drank heavily when my children were asleep at night to try and escape the pain. Eventually I found my way to healing through the Catholic Church. It has been a painful journey. I still miss Christopher. There is still a hole in our family that is Christopher-shaped. I sense it all the time. I know it will always be there.

"The doctors didn't know of a surgery to perform to heal my son at the time. But, people like me, aborting, ensure that they never will know of one. Without sick children, and mothers willing to fight for those sick children, there isn't a reason for doctors to innovate. There is no reason to care for or worry about those sick babies—not in a world where the attitude is that they shouldn't have been born in the first place!

"We women need to be strong for our children. We need to stand up for them when they can't and care for them when they are sick—even before they are born.

"Christopher didn't stop being my son because I aborted him. Christopher was a sick baby. He needed help to live. He died because of my choice. My abortion made me the mother of a dead baby. It didn't solve anything for me or my family.

"Don't let yourself be fooled into thinking there is any such thing as a moral abortion. There is no such animal in existence. I have to live with that knowledge for the rest of my life."

Charlene is not alone; many parents every year are given the advice to terminate their pregnancies because of a poor prenatal diagnosis. Aborting a child because of a bad diagnosis this far into the pregnancy is doubly difficult because this child had already been accepted into the family, making the impact of the abortion harder to grieve and to heal from. What they needed, instead of abortion, was a good doctor willing to treat both patients.

Vanna from Georgia writes:

"I was married for two years and I desperately wanted a baby after suffering a miscarriage. I was thrilled to be pregnant again. Then I got my AFP test results indicating that there was too much AFP in my bloodstream indicating a birth defect. I went for an ultrasound, which was nerve wracking because the technician was so intent on finding the problem. When she left the room without talking to me, I knew it was serious. My doctor explained that my baby probably had spina bifida and that I needed to go to a neonatal specialist to confirm the diagnosis. Spina bifida was confirmed a week or so later and the doctors explained the defect and its implications.

"They didn't know the severity of the defect, but since it involved the spinal cord there was a possibility of brain damage. There would most likely be water on the brain, paralysis, possible foot deformities. In addition to all this, it appeared that my baby's head was possibly misshapen.

"I am ultimately the person who made the decision to terminate. There was not one single person who supported me when I tried to explain why I did

not want to abort. My husband has a sister with epilepsy and he said that he couldn't voluntarily go through what he watched his parents live through. My parents didn't want to see me suffer taking care of the child. My sister, my grandmothers, and my friends, were all in agreement. I wish I had been strong enough in character to do the right thing.

"I went to the hospital's labor and delivery floor totally unprepared. After filling out the paperwork, a nurse asked me what I wanted done with the body. This was a complete shock. She said some people have funerals. Some people just discard them. Some people donate them to science. Since I was too ashamed for a funeral, I asked that the body go to a facility studying the specific birth defect.

"The labor was hell and I suspect they gave me a drug along with the inducer that makes you too ill to really be aware of what is going on. I had extreme vomiting and diarrhea which my husband had to clean up as if I were an infant. But I remember my little baby. He was long and skinny. His head looked fine. They showed me the hole in his back and the spinal cord hanging out as if to say, see you did the right thing. I wish I had held and prayed over him, but I was so, so sick and my wimp of a husband left before he emerged.

"I only got a glimpse of him, but I'll never forget it as long as I live. I think of him as Adam and I will never stop regretting that I robbed him of a chance to live, a chance to prove he was worth something.

"I went to church and cried during the entire service. I have since come to terms with my guilt and I know that this experience has made me a better and more spiritual person. But I will always regret what I did and I would change it if I could."

Vanna is living with a lifetime of guilt, wondering what might have been had she not caved into medical advice and pressure to terminate her pregnancy. The shockwaves touched Vanna and her family, who will never know the joy that little baby could have brought to them, even with his illness.

Whether the abortion is in the very earliest weeks of the pregnancy or much later, the result is the same. The woman is still a mother, but now she is the mother of a dead baby. Even when these women find healing by attending an abortion recovery program they never forget the children they aborted. They can recall their abortion like it was yesterday. Many of them name their children and have them memorialized in some way. The abortion wasn't a giant eraser that got rid of their problem; it just created many other problems in their lives. No matter what the reason was that brought them to the abortion clinic the result is the same.

While mothers and babies are at the epicenter of the abortion, they are not the only people impacted. In the next chapter, we will learn how the fathers are affected.

Chapter 5

Fatherhood Forever

When most people think of abortion, they think of the baby who is lost and the mother who made this irrevocable "choice." But fathers also experience the shockwaves of abortion and need healing. Let's take a look at the fathers' situation.

First it's important to realize that the Supreme Court decisions on Jan. 22, 1973, *Roe v.Wade* and *Doe v. Bolton*, gave zero rights to the father of the baby. It's only the mother who makes the decision to have the abortion, even if the father of the baby wants her to continue the pregnancy and will support her and his child. He is powerless to stop the abortion, so says the court! But what does that do to the father? A man has the role, by his very nature, of being the protector of his child. Imagine a father who wants a woman to have his child and he is willing to support her and the baby and yet she still goes ahead and has the abortion. Let's hear from men who had this experience.

Kyle was powerless to stop the abortion of both of his children. Here's his story:

"In 2007 my ex, Elizabeth, aborted our child after I begged her not to, and even though my pleas were from the heart, it did not matter. She went through with, it despite my pain and sadness.

"In 2008 I met Donna, an amazing woman with three kids. We fell in love, and I told her about my ex aborting our child and how deeply it hurt me. She said she could see how devastated and hurt I was from it and promised me she would never do something like that to me and that she would love to have my baby.

"She discovered she was pregnant in March 2009. At her first sonogram appointment, she told the doctor about the medicine she was taking to treat high blood pressure. He told her she could switch to a safer drug that would not hurt the baby. I was very excited that day because I have never gone through something so special with anyone, and I was happy that it was with Donna.

"When we got home, Donna said she could not have this baby. I was shocked and confused. I mentioned the other, safer drug, and she said the doctor didn't know what he was talking about. As I was thinking about our child and all the things I wanted to do with him or her, Donna made an appointment at an abortion clinic. When the day came, I went with her. Once inside, I started to cry and freak out, saying, 'I cannot be here, I cannot do this, please let's leave.' Seeing the women who had gone through with it and how out of it they were affected Donna as well. We left, and I was hopeful that maybe, just maybe, our child would be given a chance to live.

"A few days later Donna decided she was going to have a doctor prescribe her a pill that would cause her to miscarry. I begged and pleaded with Donna not to do it. She said she had no choice because of her high blood pressure medication and the impact it would have on the baby. I stayed with her through her at-home abortion because I needed to be with our child, even as he or she died.

"As weeks went by, I started to think about our child, the life he or she would not have, and all the things I would miss out on. I started to feel a sense of how I failed to protect my child from death. Then I would see Donna being affectionate with her kids and that hurt and made me jealous. I started to become withdrawn and started to resent Donna for placing this hurt on me again. I loved Donna so much, and I felt so betrayed by a woman I deeply loved and wanted to spend the rest of my life with.

"As time went on our arguing became more frequent and eventually became physical, with me having this deep hurt and rage towards Donna. I know I loved her with all of my heart, but I was so very angry with her for doing what she did.

"A year later, Donna was pregnant again. I told her I could not go through with another abortion. But this time, Donna wanted to have the baby. I was confused—why did she want this baby and not the first one? It turned out not to matter, as Donna miscarried this pregnancy.

"I later learned that Donna was still legally married when she got pregnant in 2009. This made me even more angry and hurt that our child was aborted so she could save face, spare her ex's feelings, and not face any ridicule from her family. I felt angrier with Donna because I felt she lied to me and left me on my own to deal with this pain. Death is irreversible and no one can undo it once it is done.

"There is not a day that goes by that I do not think of the kids I lost, especially the two whose mothers made the decision to kill them without even considering what I wanted. I feel as if I am cursed. Why has this happened to me?

"In 2011, Elizabeth contacted me, asking for forgiveness. She was pregnant again and even though *she said she did not want to have a child with the man she was involved with, she was going through with the pregnancy because she had seen how the abortion of our child had devastated me. This hurt me. Due to my pain and the loss of my child, she was going to give another man what I wanted: A child, a life. I cut off contact with her.*

"Both Elizabeth's and Donna's abortions made me feel hopeless, hurt, betrayed, confused, unworthy, and unloved. Those are tough things to deal with, and I felt alone. I did not speak to anyone about it.

"I know many people say that abortion destroys relationships. I was trying so hard for that to not be Donna's and my fate but in 2013 our relationship ended. I have no contact with her or the kids even though I treated the kids as my own, and they looked up to me as their dad. Losing them hurts me every day.

"I have been to counseling sessions numerous times, I attend church regularly and I meditate. But still, there is not a day that goes by that I do not wish my kids were here. There have been times I have wished to not live this life anymore. Fighting depression has become a daily battle. I don't think people care about the feelings of the man when his child is aborted, especially when he does not want the abortion. Society cares only about the woman and all I have to say is that it takes two to create."

You can see how having his fatherhood aborted wounded Kyle very deeply. It also affected how he related to the women in his life, the very women he thought would be the mothers of his children. You see, even though he has been through counseling, attends church and meditates, he constantly thinks of the children he lost to abortion. The shockwaves continue to impact him.

Here's Jason, another dad who lost a child to abortion.

"Abortion was one of those things I thought would never touch my life. In fact, I really didn't even have an opinion about it. But it came as a big surprise when I had to face the issue personally. First, I was surprised by my response to it, and second, at the profound impact an abortion would have on my life.

"I had a happy childhood in Pennsylvania and signed up for the Air Force when I was still a junior in high school. I left for boot camp right after graduation.

"I was assigned to Andrews Air Force Base in Washington D.C. I quickly made new friends and discovered the joys of partying. All through high school I never even had a single drink, so I broke loose and partied hard. One night I met a girl and had my first sexual encounter. We ended up dating for a couple of years.

"When my girlfriend broke up with me for some other guy, it crushed my self-esteem. I spent a lot of my time just sitting around drinking. I also became promiscuous and would sleep with anyone who would show interest. I started oversleeping a lot and got into trouble for being late for work. I no longer enjoyed my job, and I had lost myself in alcohol and sexual addiction.

"When I left the Air Force, I returned to my home town and got a job in retail. I soon ran into Andrea, a childhood friend whom I hadn't seen in years. She had just moved back from New York and had a five-month-old daughter. Andrea and I started hanging out together and our relationship quickly became sexual. I bonded well with her daughter and before long, we decided to get an apartment together.

"It didn't take long for me to realize I enjoyed family life, so I asked Andrea to marry me, and she agreed. We didn't make much money, but I worked hard to support Andrea and her daughter and was getting frequent promotions at work. Then one day I came home from work and Andrea told me she was pregnant. I was thrilled! Her daughter was almost three years old and now she'd have a baby brother or sister. I told everyone in my family and at work that I was going to be a daddy.

"At first, Andrea seemed happy about the pregnancy. But after a few weeks, things started to change. She was saying things like, 'I'm not sure if we're ready for another child' and, 'We can't afford to have a baby right now.' I tried to assure her that we'd be fine. I offered to get a second job so I could better support her and the kids. But her doubts and fears increased and finally she told me she was considering abortion. Suddenly, I was terrified. I had never given much thought to abortion and hadn't even considered the possibility of aborting our own child. For me, that just wasn't an option. I was excited about being a father and didn't want to lose this child.

"Our discussions turned into arguments. Our arguments turned into fights. It was impossible to have a civilized conversation about it. We were on opposite ends of the spectrum. Every time I tried to plead with her to keep our child, she would tell me it wasn't my decision, that it was her body and her choice. I even offered that if she just had the baby, I would raise it on my own. I became so desperate that I went to a lawyer to see if I could stop her. Unfortunately, he told me there was no legal action I could take. As a father, I had no rights until the child was born. I thought it was ironic that a man could go to jail for not paying child support, but could do nothing to protect his unborn child. The only hope I had was that Andrea couldn't afford to get an abortion and I wasn't about to pay for it.

"It was on February 25, 1995 that my life changed forever. Andrea had gone to the clinic and had the abortion while I was at work. Her sister paid for the procedure and was the one who told me it was done. The last thing I remember after hearing the news was lying in the parking lot of a bar screaming at the top of my lungs. I have no recollection of how I got home or how many days passed before I moved back in with my parents.

"The next several months were just a blur. Andrea and I didn't talk for a long time, and when we did, the conversations were heated. But somehow we worked things out and I moved back in with her. But things would never be the same. I started having anger issues, had trouble staying focused on my job, and would often break down and cry from depression. Andrea also seemed depressed at times and started exhibiting reckless behaviors. Eventually our relationship collapsed and she moved out.

"My depression was getting worse and I was angry all the time at everything and everyone. I was drinking heavily and started using drugs. I was also having trouble sleeping at night and my job performance began to suffer. I was stricken with panic attacks that seemed to come for no reason and without warning. I decided to see a psychiatrist before I lost all control. He identified the fact that my problems stemmed from the abortion, diagnosed me with severe depression and borderline psychosis, and prescribed medications for depression, anxiety, and sleeplessness. At his recommendation, I also took a three-month leave of absence from work and entered a hospital treatment program.

"All the medications seemed to just cloud my head instead of making me feel better, so I continued using illegal drugs and alcohol on top of the medications. In the hospital, I was surrounded by people with severe emotional problems all day long, which didn't seem to help.

"During my counseling sessions and group therapies, we talked about my emotions and how to control them, but never targeted the source of my problems—the abortion. No one seemed to understand or know how to help me deal with my loss. Since I wasn't working, I was quickly running out of money. I pawned everything I owned just to buy my medications and support my drug habits. I also found myself in and out of meaningless relationships.

"Finally, I reached a point where I felt there was no hope. I figured no one would ever understand, that I must be crazy for even feeling a sense of loss, and that I would never get better. Life was no longer worth living. So I sat at my dining room table with the last bottle of sleeping pills I had. 'This will be easy' I thought to myself. I would just swallow all these pills, lay down, fall asleep, and never wake up.

"I poured the pills into my hand and as I raised them to put them in my mouth, I was suddenly overcome by a feeling of intense warmth over my entire body and complete peace. My mouth was open and my hand was only a few inches away, yet there I sat, frozen, staring at the wall. All of a sudden, with an earthquake-like shudder, the pills flew out of my hand and I collapsed to the floor sobbing like a child. For the next 45 minutes or so, I laid there on the floor crying, trying to figure out what had just happened. Then, in a moment, I felt compelled to grab the phone book. I didn't know what I was looking for, but I flipped it open and right there on the first page I came to was an ad with large print asking if I was 'Looking for a new home?' It was an ad for a church.

"To this day I believe God reached down and comforted me at a time when I needed Him most, even though I wasn't looking for Him."

Jason joined the church, and his healing journey began. Wanting to reach out to other men impacted by the shockwaves of abortion, he began to minister to others in his situation and he created the Men's Healing Network and founded the Fatherhood Forever Foundation, which now is part of the Silent No More Awareness Campaign. You can find more information at *www.Fatherhoodforever.org.*

Here's another post-abortive dad, John, who tried too late to stop the abortion of his child.

"I first met Janet in a softball league. She was a great pitcher. We hit it off right away. We were very attracted to one another and after a lot of mutual flirting I finally got the nerve to ask her out. I knew she already had a child from a previous relationship, but I was so taken by her that didn't bother me a bit. Janet just started a new job because she wanted to get her life together so she could be a role model for her 4-year-old daughter. We progressed to regular dating and eventually we began to have sex. I was falling deeper in love with her and grew attached to her daughter as well.

"When we had sex we would always use birth control. There was one night we went out together to hear a local band. We were dancing and having a great time. When we got back to her apartment we just threw caution to the wind and had unprotected sex. I am not sure why we did that. I think we were just caught up in the joy of being together, of the love and passion we shared.

"A few weeks later she told me she missed her period. My first reaction was fear, but I also felt excited about being a dad. I was in love with Janet and hoped we could work it out. Unfortunately, Janet had a different reaction.

"Janet was already a single parent. She just started a new job she loved. She was embarrassed to be in this situation again, and felt that she couldn't face family and friends with another unplanned pregnancy. Janet felt stupid, foolish, and angry. I told her that I would help her, and that we could get married. She didn't want to marry because of the pregnancy, and I don't think she trusted that I would be there for her down the line (she had been down that road before).

"That's when Janet first said it: 'I want to get an abortion.' I felt sick in my stomach. I felt like this is my kid, too, and I wanted to have this baby. But I was also scared of losing Janet. Maybe Janet sensed my fear, or maybe I wasn't strong enough in opposition—maybe it wouldn't have mattered, I don't know. I knew that she was set on getting that abortion.

"I decided to support Janet in her decision, pay for the abortion and drive her to the abortion center.

"The day of the abortion was warm and gray, with a very fine mist falling from the sky. We drove silently to the abortion center and parked in the lot. 'Do you want me to come in with you?' I asked. She told me to wait in the car, and to be truthful I was relieved not to go into that place.

"As I was sitting there alone in my car it began to hit me what was about to happen. How can I sit here and let this happen to my baby—that's my son or daughter they are going to kill! I jumped out of the car and ran into the building. The receptionist told me that Janet was in the procedure room and that I could take a seat and wait. I blew past her and after bursting through a few doors came upon a scene that burned into my mind and haunted me for months after.

"As I entered that room, Janet screamed out 'John, what are you doing?' The doctor looked at me and smiled, 'John we are just finishing up, everything went fine.' I looked at Janet; she was white as a ghost and crying. Our baby had just been killed! I was unable to stop it. I even paid for it to happen! It was a living nightmare. I stormed out of the building, knocking over some chairs and a trash can in my rage. We drove home in silence, both in shock.

"In the days after that nightmare in the abortion center, I was filled with rage at the abortionist and at Janet. How could they do this to my child! Was this the only way? Why couldn't we work this out and save our baby! Why was this child sacrificed because of our stupidity! I stopped seeing Janet. I was too filled with rage, anger, and grief to even look at her.

"For the next four months I slept very little. I would lie awake at night and stare at the ceiling, reliving that day. When I slept I would dream of that same horrible scene where I would break into the abortion procedure room, but in these nightmares I would find my dead baby in pieces. I would wake from this terror filled with rage and grief— how could I let this happen, how could I have been so weak, so evil. But my grief quickly transformed into a seething rage at Janet, the abortionist, and the abortion business that took the life of my child. I was sure that I would never escape this nightmare.

"I returned to work, and looking back now, the routine of work during those months saved my life.

At least during the day I could stay focused and escape my private hell—but at night, the demons returned to torture me till dawn. I would get a few hours of sleep if I was lucky, and just try to get through each day.

"After four months of this hell, a ray of light shown into my darkness. I continued to go to church off and on after the abortion. I would sit in the back like a zombie, waiting for the Lord to strike me with lightning—I was actually praying that he would take my life. I also prayed for the strength not to take my own life. But God gave me a road to travel that would save my life and much more.

"This particular Sunday, near the close of the service, a speaker got up and talked about a healing weekend for people involved in abortion called Rachel's Vineyard Retreats. A few days later, I called the ministry and registered for the next weekend retreat.

"I found my healing during that weekend retreat. If I remained consumed with hatred and thoughts of revenge, I would stay locked in that prison of pain and possibly hurt someone, or more likely, myself. No one could get close to me, and I wouldn't let anyone in. Now my wall of rage and hatred were being dismantled, and my heart was softening and the tears could flow. I could face the searing pain beneath my rage, the deep grief at participating in the death of my child. But I was also filled with great consolation, and I now live with the hope that when my life is ended, I will meet my precious child."

John, like many other men, was going along with what his girlfriend said she wanted. Unfortunately for John, he came to the realization of what was happening too late, and tried unsuccessfully to save the life of his child. Thankfully, John was able to come to terms with his grief by attending a Rachel's Vineyard retreat. These retreats provide healing for men and women hurting after their abortions. You can go to the website *www.RachelsVineyard.org* for more information.

Some men tell their girlfriends or wives that it is up to them and they will support them in whatever they decide. That is a cowardly response! Most women will take that as a signal that the man doesn't want the baby or isn't ready to be a father. Women instinctively want the man in their lives to embrace the fact that they are having a baby. Even in difficult circumstances, if the man acts thrilled and excited and says 'don't worry we can get through this,' then the couple immediately takes a path towards having the baby and figuring it out.

Here are stories from some of these ambivalent men, who left it up to their girlfriends to decide. Even these men suffer from regret.

Paul Marshall found himself at Planned Parenthood looking for parenting classes when he and his high school sweetheart discovered she was pregnant a second time. The first pregnancy ended in abortion and this time, they wanted a different outcome. Let's see what happened to them.

"When my girlfriend and I found ourselves facing a second unplanned pregnancy in high school, we went to Planned Parenthood to find out about taking classes to prepare ourselves for our new role as parents. We had already lost one child to a brutal second trimester saline abortion. That decision was made for us by our family and it had a major impact on us both.

"But as we know now, Planned Parenthood has nothing to do with helping people plan to be parents. When we asked about taking classes, a clinic staffer told us that was the most foolish thing we could do and that we should have an abortion

because in the first trimester what was growing in her womb was not yet a human being. She showed us diagrams of blobs of tissue and said that's all our child was. Any religious objections we might harbor wouldn't even come into play, she said, because our child was not yet human.

"We left that clinic unsure what to do. When she said our baby was not yet human, we believed her. This was new information we had never heard before. A week later, mostly out of fear of what our parents would say about a second pregnancy, we went back to this clinic—on Genesee Street in Syracuse, NY—paid our money up front and she had the abortion. It took about an hour total. Whatever they did to my girlfriend out of my sight, we never talked about. Never. Within a few minutes of walking out the door, I realized we had made a huge mistake. We walked in complete silence until we got to the interstate overpass and then she burst into tears. I can still see the look on her face to this day. And my heart turned as stone cold as the cement of that overpass. Our relationship ended in bitter hostility about nine months later.

"I was a senior in high school when I found my faith and began attending church. It was then that I came to understand how wrong it was to do what we had done. I became angry and depressed. I dealt with the pain through massive alcohol consumption.

"Looking back, I can honestly say that the clinic staffer was trying to coerce us into abortion. Ultimately the decision was ours, but if she had not lied to us, or if we had stumbled into a pregnancy resource center instead of Planned Parenthood, my child might be in my life today. I have a beautiful family now—a wife, three children, two grandchildren—and I know that my high school girlfriend also has a very nice family, but to this day it still

hurts that we each lost a lifetime with two of our children. I did complete an abortion recovery program called, "Healing A Father's Heart" and it was one of the best investments of time I've ever made because it gave me the tools I needed to cope with my loss.

"I am now the president and executive director of Care Net Pregnancy Center of Central New York, and we are committed to educating individuals with the truth about fetal development. I find it ironic that pro-abortion people always falsely accuse pregnancy care centers of lying to women—about the emotional aftereffects of abortion, about the physical risks, about its link to breast cancer. And yet, I was lied to at Planned Parenthood and we know they are still lying about the humanity of the child in the womb. But behind closed doors, these doctors and nurses and technicians know exactly what they are doing and to whom. I can't believe what they are allowed to get away with, and I can't believe we are paying for it."

Notice that for Paul, once he came to the realization of what he had done—destroyed the life of his children—he turned to alcohol just to numb the pain he felt as the shockwaves continued to reverberate. He also buried his feelings deep down and never confronted the pain for many years until he heard there were other men who felt like he did and that he could confront those painful memories and come to terms with them in an abortion-recovery program for men.

Stephen was living with his girlfriend when she became pregnant and now regrets that he did not stand up for her or his unborn child. Let's read what he has to say.

"Within a few years after Roe v. Wade *legalized abortion in our country, I was away from the sacraments and the Catholic faith, living with a woman*

outside of marriage. It wasn't long before she told me she was pregnant with our child.

"I did as many men do in these situations. I did not tell her that I would stand by her and our child and that she should have the baby. On the contrary, I told her that I would support her in whatever decision she made, and then I proceeded to tell her all the reasons why the timing of the pregnancy was not good.

"Clearly, I let her know it was her responsibility, not mine. Years later I realized she had the abortion for me. After all, women are intuitive and I am sure she realized that if I wanted the baby, I would have said so.

"So she aborted the baby—for me. She never said it was for me, but it was for me. I didn't even go with her to the abortion clinic. Of course back then, there was no real pro-life movement to tell the truth about abortion. It was a simple medical procedure in my mind. Again in hindsight, I realize that I was just exhibiting more cowardly behavior and rationalizing later on that maybe if I had gone with her, I would have stopped her or rescued her at the last minute. Maybe, but in hindsight and in all honesty, I doubt it.

"Not long after the abortion, I began to realize she had changed. When I asked her about it, she had no hesitation in telling me that what we did was wrong; that the abortion was wrong. I told her I felt guilty, too, and that she was right. It was wrong.

"I then made arrangements for us to go to confession and see a priest friend of my family. After the confession, we started living the faith again, but that was short-lived and we fell back to where we were before. After a few years, we parted amicably.

"More than 25 years later, I was in the seminary and deep into my pro-life work. I found myself sidewalk counseling in front of the same abortion mill where my former girlfriend had gone for her abortion decades before, Metropolitan Medical Associates in Englewood, N.J. This one particular morning, I was speaking to a young man, telling him what I had told many men I've encountered outside abortion mills: 'She is having this abortion for you, and unless you go in and tell her you don't want her to have the abortion, she thinks you want her to have the abortion.' Twice among the many times I have said this, two men have gone in and saved their babies. On this occasion, something different happened. I heard a voice inside me say the same words Nathaniel said to David to convict him of his deadly sin: 'You are that man.' At that instant, I realized that this is exactly what I had done to my girlfriend decades before.

"Being convicted now not just of killing my child, but also wounding my girlfriend, I asked my spiritual director if I could look my girlfriend up and apologize to her for my sin. I was given permission and not long after, we met for lunch.

"Although she knew I was in the seminary, I had not seen her in years. I immediately told her I had reached out to her to apologize for not standing by her and not standing up for our baby. I told her that I came to know that she had not wanted to have the abortion but did it for me. Her eyes began to tear up and I knew immediately that I was correct and that she had needed to hear this, maybe had even waited to hear this for years. I continued to tell her everything I had come to understand including that our baby was in heaven. I told her, hoping she would not mind, that I named our baby Mary and that it brought me comfort over the years to be able to ask Mary for her intercession *and help. At that point she said, 'We have two babies in heaven.' Startled and not being able to think of anything else, I responded, 'You had two abortions?' She answered, 'No, I never told you, I was pregnant with twins.'*

"She had carried this guilty secret for years. How difficult this must have been for her and how much more difficult the abortion must have been. I apologized to her, opening up a flood of grace in her healing process and mine. I realized that I now needed to heal from my complicity in wounding my girlfriend and in the death of my second child whom we named Thomas.

"The abortion sin was an impediment to my ordination as a priest, but, as with many circumstances within the Church, after due investigation, a dispensation can be obtained. I was a recipient of such a dispensation, which allowed me to continue my pro-life work and was ordained to the priesthood.

"When I tell my story, as I did at the foot of the Supreme Court in January 2005, as the first male witness of the Silent No More Awareness Campaign, and again in January 2016, I always identify with 'Everyman' and apologize to all women who have suffered from abortion, especially those who are victims of men who have done what I did. It is so important that men stand up for women and their babies and, when prudent, apologize for not being better men."

The Stephen in this story is Father Stephen Imbarrato, a pastoral associate for Priests for Life who continues to be a voice for the Silent No More Awareness Campaign.

Men who agree with their wives or girlfriends that abortion is the best choice also suffer regret down the line. We know from many of the testimonies from women in these circumstances that they came to regret their abortion and in fact, resented the baby's father for supporting them in the abortion decision. What effect does this have on the men? Let's take a look.

Pat from Ontario, Canada said this:

"I lost my faith as a teen. I didn't believe in anything. The world had its influence. It said one was stupid to believe in God. Religion was a joke.

"I didn't have much money so when my 17-year-old girlfriend became pregnant I talked to a friend about it, and he showed me an ad in the newspaper for an abortion clinc. She was confused about how to cope with the situation. We decided to answer the ad and the outcome was the death of our child. We did it a second time. The same abortionist preformed a second abortion. While my girlfriend was on the table he said to her, 'So once was not enough!'

"My girlfriend had two abortions before we got married. I never gave it any thought. We only cared about ourselves. We were self-indulgent and of the world. Eventually, our marriage fell apart.

"The breakup began a spiritual awakening that changed my life on a physical and spiritual level. I wondered, 'Where did I go wrong?' The separation and the hurting were good in that it made me realize that I needed to get back to my roots. I returned to my church and through the Knights of Columbus became active in pro-life. I realized there's nothing without God!

"I am responsible for the death of two of my children. I came to realize this by returning to my relationship with God, who is Truth. I felt guilt, shame, and regret and wondered how God could ever forgive such a thing. I felt like a monster! I killed my own kids! I had treated my children as objects. I had cut them off like a wart.

"Eventually, I was led to ask for forgiveness. The only way I could survive was with God. I came to

know that He was in charge. I became aware of my children who died through abortion. I spiritually baptized them and named them, Pat and Sam.

"I share my testimony in the hope that it will help someone else to know that abortion is wrong and that there is nothing without God.

"Today, I pray daily for the unborn. I have become a responsible person, active in my church and community. I now do what is right. I stand up for the unborn and any other vulnerable person. I know I am forgiven by God and my children."

Notice that both Pat and his girlfriend thought abortion would be an easy out. They were only concerned about themselves and in the moment. But you can see when they married, what they thought was going to be a happy life ended because of the guilt they felt over destroying the life of two of their children. Abortion took away the problem of an unexpected pregnancy, but the shockwaves in its wake overwhelmed them and they divorced.

Eric from New York shared:

"I am a Christian, a husband, a father, and I work as a hairdresser in New York City. And I am torn apart by the fact that I did not stop the abortion of my precious daughter.

"I began telling everyone, co-workers, clients, and friends, how important two days were in my future. The first was January 23, the date my then three-year-old daughter would premiere as a Gap model. It was going to be an exciting day to see her bigger than life in store windows all over Manhattan. The other was May 7, my daughter Emmanuelle's due date. But before either of those dates arrived, my wife and I went for a sonogram and learned that Emmanuelle had a rare brain anomaly, which would cause seizures and clenched

fists. The doctor was very upset that he had to give us the news that our daughter was not perfect. He said 'we'll talk about options tomorrow morning,' but we never talked about options.

"Instead, on January 15, my wife and I let the doctors kill Emmanuelle. I sat nearby quietly praying while the doctor inserted a huge needle into my wife's belly as she lay sedated, and injected a solution straight into the heart of my precious daughter, killing her instantly. Afterward I thought, how can I ask God to bless me after what I have done?*

"When my wife went to the doctor for her post-abortion checkup, she learned that the doctor had taken a picture of Emmanuelle after she was aborted. I suppose it is a picture of her lying dead on the table shortly after the delivery. I've never looked at the picture. I still cannot believe that my wife brought that picture home.*

"I don't know if my marriage can ever be restored. I look at my wife and am reminded of the sin we committed. Though I love my two beautiful children, I am constantly reminded that one is missing. How will I tell my children about their sister in heaven? Will I ever be free of the guilt and shame? I look forward to the day when I can ever so humbly ask her for forgiveness.*

"There are constant reminders of what I have done, and I find myself wondering if I will ever get back on the path where, at the end, I will be met by God saying, 'Well done good and faithful servant.' For now, I am committed to speaking out in the hope of waking up the medical community and to reaching out to other victims of abortion, particularly the husbands and fathers. Maybe by helping them I can help myself."*

In Eric's story you see he and his wife being led by the doctor down the path to abortion. The doctor felt bad having to tell them their daughter wasn't going to be perfect, but how many of us have been born with physical problems that we have overcome to lead happy and productive lives? Also, how many of these fetal diagnoses prove to be wrong? I have heard from many couples that were given a poor fetal diagnosis and didn't abort, later delivering a perfectly healthy baby. Medical tests can be wrong, but Eric and his wife will never know how Emmanuelle's life would have been, and they have to live with the guilt of having destroyed the life of their unborn child. The shockwaves of abortion gain strength when the child lost was a wanted child.

Now let's take a look at men who are told their wife or girlfriend is pregnant and they react by asserting, "we can't afford to have a baby right now," or "I am not ready to be a Dad," or "I have to finish school." These are the men who pressure women to abort, some in subtle ways and some even resorting to threats of violence or abandonment if the mothers try to choose life.

David from Indiana had this to say:

"We had an abortion because we thought another child at the time would have complicated our lives and were not sure we could afford it. Upon finding out we were pregnant, I was actually excited about having another child. A few weeks later my wife said that she did not want to have the baby if I was not there to support her. I had just finished graduate school and was working long hours at my first job out of school. I remember thinking at the time, 'it is her decision' and wanted to support her, especially knowing how driven I was to succeed in my career.

"Going to the abortion clinic was like going to any doctor's office. There was a survey we filled out on demographics and reasons for getting the abortion. No one ever tried to talk us out of it or offer other options. After the interview we sat

in the waiting room with ten or so other people. Again, just like any doctor's office with magazines. They called my wife in and I waited, not sure how long. I read magazines while I waited for her to be done. When she was finished she was quiet and never talked with me about what happened. I never asked her. We were quiet on the way home and that evening. I remember her eventually crying uncontrollably that night, and that was the first time I really started feeling regret.

"The abortion was a turning point in our lives. I threw myself into work and ended up supporting her even less than before. We both turned to alcohol, she more than I, and suffered from depression for many years. This started a cycle that ended up with my selfishness occupying my time with little room for the daughter we had or for our relationship. We ended up getting divorced about six years after the abortion, after several attempts at counseling. I was denying my own issues with alcohol and other addictive behaviors. I fell into my own extended battle with depression. Our daughter also suffered, without knowing about the abortion, as she was reacting to my inability to be an effective father. To this day, we are still estranged. She did find out about the abortion and blames me for it.

"When I finally realized my life was unmanageable, I reached out to God with the help of some friends. That journey helped reconcile me with the Church, and I was eventually able to confess the sin of participating in an abortion and receive absolution. That process has started me on the road to healing and now I can focus on atonement.

"I am silent no more because men need to know they will suffer from abortion. They unjustly place a scar on the woman by making her go through an abortion, and it is not just the woman's decision—half the child's DNA is theirs."

Once again, what was thought to be a quick fix to their financial difficulties ended being a problem that haunted this couple for many years. They never spoke about the abortion with each other but began abusing alcohol to numb their pain. Even David's relationship with his daughter changed when she found out about the abortion. She blamed him and she, too, was hurt because she has a sibling she will never know. Sibling survivors of abortion experience the shockwaves.

David from San Antonio, Texas wrote:

"I participated in my first abortion when my girlfriend, who I was having an adulterous affair with, became pregnant with another man because I would not leave my wife for her. She informed me of her crisis pregnancy to see what my reaction would be. I knew I could not allow myself to be the father of an illegitimate child. However, since I wanted to continue my physical relationship with this young woman I told her I would be the man the baby's father could not be, and helped her with her decision to abort the unwanted child.

"I remember everything about that hot, ugly, humid, dark summer day. I watched as she slowly walked from the procedure room of the abortion clinic. Before we got in the car she started to vomit and she told me she had acute abdominal pain. She was bleeding, but they told her that was to be expected. All I wanted to do was escape and get away from her and the entire situation. I felt fearful yet liberated; I realized how low I could actually go. I fell into acute depression, alcoholism, and increased my drug use. I had multiple adulterous affairs with depravity of all sorts. I had a drive for money and power. I felt the wealthier and more powerful I became, the more distance I could put between me and my past. No matter how well I dressed and who I pretended to be, my hideous past was right there with me. In my despair I had violent mood swings.

"One year later, when she became pregnant again, this time it was my child. My fury was unparalleled. I viciously dragged her to an abortion clinic that she went running out of. I thought she was lying about being pregnant to trap me into leaving my wife and marrying her. The reality was I did not want to share or sacrifice anything, my time, my money with anyone, not even a baby.

"I remember that day. The abortion clinic was packed with women; she was crying, I did not react. When the baby was dead, I dropped her at her townhouse, returned to my house and asked my wife what was for dinner. I tried to pretend that everything was normal. It wasn't long after that before I hit rock bottom and checked myself into a rehab center.

"When I was released, I knew that I needed more help. I immediately went to confession with a Catholic priest. It took three consecutive days to complete my confession. But I still thought I knew better than God. Even though I had received absolution for my sins, I couldn't accept God's forgiveness. It wasn't until a year and-a-half later that God blessed me with the grace to finally accept His mercy and begin this long and painful process of healing.

"Today, with the healing I found at a Rachel's Vineyard retreat and everything that has been part of God's healing process for me I now have the peace that surpasses all understanding and through this JOY, I am willing to BE SILENT NO MORE!"

David wasn't even thinking about the woman and how she felt. He had no compassion for her nor did he care about the baby. He used abortion to hide his adulterous affair. But all the money, the powerful job, and his success didn't make him happy. The guilt eventually crept in and drugs, alcohol, and depression became part of his life until he hit rock bottom and then reached out for help. David eventually told his wife about the abortions and the affairs and they attended a Rachel's Vineyard retreat together. She forgave David for almost allowing the shockwaves to overwhelm their family, and David has learned to forgive himself. We will hear more from David's son, Daniel, in a later chapter.

Dr. Ney, the Canadian psychiatrist we met earlier in the book, has researched the effects of abortions on men and women for more than four decades. Here is what he has to say about men and abortion:

"Fathers have been overlooked and underrated for years. The consequence of that is that they don't involve themselves or take responsibility for the family the way they should. Abortion damages a man's self-esteem. They might think, 'I am a father. I should be able to look after my child, but I have no legal right to do so.' Fathers take their cues from that. If a baby can be aborted without their awareness or consent, it damages their manhood. I think the damage to men is just as severe as the damage to women.

"There are men who coerce their partners into having an abortion, threatening to leave if their partner does not agree to abort the child. This is effective because so many women have grown up without fathers. The tragedy, so often, is that she'll abort and he'll leave anyhow. This increasing hostility between the sexes is enjoyed by Planned Parenthood. It's exactly what Satan wanted: Men and women so angry with each other that they won't have children."

Scholarly research also has been done by Catherine Coyle, Ph.D., Vincent Rue, Ph.D. and Priscilla Coleman, Ph.D. regarding men and abortion. Here are some of the things they have discovered about men and abortion:

1. Many men describe abortion as the worst experience of their lives.

2. Men experience a variety of emotions after abortion, such as anxiety, grief, depression, powerlessness, guilt, rage, and anger.

3. Men tend to defer the abortion decision to their partners.

4. Men may repress their own emotions in an attempt to support their partners.

5. Men's relationships may be strained after an abortion.

6. Men may experience sexual problems after an abortion experience.

7. Men's masculine identity may be threatened by an abortion experience.

8. Men experience post-traumatic stress disorder after an abortion experience.

This research backs up what the men of Silent No More have experienced. More information on this research can be found at *www.standapart.org*.

Abortion impacts men in a variety of ways. Some try to medicate themselves by abusing drugs and alcohol just to forget about the pain. Others become workaholics and immerse themselves in their careers. Other addictive behaviors include addictions to gambling and pornography.

Whether the father of the baby advocated for the abortion, was ambivalent, or tried to stop the abortion, all experienced problems afterward. Abortion attacks the very nature of a man to be the protector of his family. In his role as father, he is entrusted with the care and well-being of his children, and his number one priority is to love and nurture them. Violating this fundamental law of nature can later weaken men in their vocation as husband, father, and leader. As you can see, the shockwaves men experience after abortion not only impact them but also how they fill their roles in society. How different would our world be if abortion hadn't weakened these men?

Chapter Six

Mourning Lost Grandchildren

Grandparents tend to say the same thing: They had no idea that complete, unconditional love would fill their hearts the first time they set eyes on a new grandson or granddaughter.

Similarly, grandparents of aborted children had no idea how deep the wound would be when that grandson or granddaughter was lost to abortion. They experience the shockwaves of abortion in unique ways, depending on their involvement.

Grandparents can play many different roles in an abortion. They may have condoned it, or coerced it, or opposed it. They may not have known about it for days, months or even years or decades later. But these abortions leave a hole in their hearts, no matter what their involvement.

Let's take a look at some grandmothers who insisted on the abortion, participated in the abortion, or had no idea until after it was too late to learn if their experiences have any similarities.

Parents who never knew about their daughter's abortion experience a wide range of emotions when they learn about their lost grandchild.

When Nancy Tanner decided to go public about her abortion regret, she knew she had to tell her family, including her mother, Mary Brindle, about the abortion she had twenty years earlier.

Mary recalls that conversation:

"We were in the car after Nancy picked me up at BWI Airport in Baltimore and we had stopped for lunch. Before we left the car, Nancy told me about the abortion. We just sat in the car and cried. I asked her why she hadn't come to me, and she said she knew what my response would have been. She knew I would try to talk her out of it. I asked her how she found herself in that situation and why she thought she had no other choice. Nancy said that she was 34 years old with two small daughters from her previous marriage and the father of this baby said it was her choice and he would pay for the abortion. Nancy felt too ashamed to confide in me. It was during this conversation that I realized I had lost a grandchild. That child was my grandchild. I would have done anything to save that baby, if I had known."

Notice that Nancy felt too embarrassed to come to her mother and the father of her baby did not stand up for his child. Instead, he paid for the abortion. Nancy was a school teacher and her colleagues all told her that abortion was her best solution to this problem. She felt like she had no other choice. It took Nancy several decades to even talk to her mom about the abortion. But ultimately Nancy and her mom were able to acknowledge and honor this lost child and grandchild.

Jacquie Stalnaker was afraid of being rejected by her parents if she told them about her abortion.

"My parents didn't know for fifteen years after I had my abortion. I felt they would disown me. After the abortion, I changed. I went from happy-go-lucky Jacquie, always doing something for someone, to what my mother called a wicked little brat. I had a very short fuse. They saw what was

happening to me and they urged me to speak to someone at my church.

"One weekend, after I had gone home to West Virginia to visit my parents, I was loading my car for the drive back. My mother was saying, again, that something was going on with me and I blurted out, 'I had an abortion. What do you think is wrong with me?' That was the first real release for me, and I got in my car and drove off.

"We didn't speak for two weeks, until I went home again. I begged my mom to talk to me about it and she said 'I'm never going to talk to you about this.' My dad was more willing to listen.

"After I told my parents, I was talking to priests about it and I was going to a Rachel's Vineyard retreat. Then they got very excited. My mom knew that part of the retreat weekend was naming the baby and she asked how I was going to choose a name. I told her I would pray about it and when the name Lilly came to me, I called and told my parents. The next day I received a beautiful bouquet of roses and white lilies, with a card from them that said, 'We are proud of you and we are with you and Lilly.' That was a pivotal moment.

"My mother wanted to be a wife and mother, and she did that. She wanted that for me, too. Three months after I got married, I had a miscarriage, a little boy I named Justin Nathaniel. It was the last time I was able to conceive. My mother is disappointed she has no grandchildren from me."

Jacquie's mom was disappointed not to have a grandchild from her daughter and until her death in 2017, only acknowledged Lilly with the bouquet.

Now let's take a look at some mothers who took their daughters for what they thought was a simple solution to a problem pregnancy. After all, our culture leads us to believe that a woman can have an abortion today and go back to work or school tomorrow, no big deal. Or is it a really big deal?

Karen Cross and her mom Betty Fralich shared:

Betty: "When Karen told me she was pregnant, those were words I never expected to hear from my teenage daughter. I wondered, what I had done wrong. But I saw that we had a problem and we were going to fix it. I had money saved from my job, and I kept Karen out of school one day and we went off to the abortion clinic. I'll never forget the sadness I felt as she left the waiting room. But after it was over, we never talked about it. I totally blocked it out and I told Karen, we don't have to think about it anymore. Karen got pregnant again and got married and had the baby, my granddaughter Brandy. Then she had a second abortion in the midst of a divorce but she didn't tell me about it.

"Years later I was watching a Christian TV show and they mentioned Karen's abortion. I was the one who took her by the hand and took her to the abortion clinic. I was mainly worried about me and what people were going to think. But after seeing that program, I was transfixed. I didn't know about Karen's nightmares and the alcohol and the suicidal thoughts. I hadn't seen or felt her heartbreak. I sobbed and I mourned the loss of my grandchildren."

As you can see, Betty thought the abortion was a quick fix to her teenage daughter's pregnancy and there was no need to talk about it further. How did that silence affect Karen? She had to stuff those feelings of regret deep inside her and she used alcohol to numb her pain. It took Karen many years to seek healing from her abortion and then more years until she and her mother could acknowledge her pain and recognize that a child was lost. Betty now mourns her grandchild and both she and Karen speak out so that others will not have to go through what they did.

Karen Reynoso had four abortions within a four-year period, beginning when she was 19 and working in construction. Her mom, Miriam Kirk, went with her for the first two abortions.

Miriam says: "I was pregnant at 16 and I married the father. By 21, I had four children, and by 25, I thought of myself as an old lady. I had given up my youth and I wanted to save Karen from that. She was a little wild in her ways and I didn't feel she was equipped to be a mother. Thinking back, I could have stepped up and done something. That's one of my regrets. If we had walked into a pregnancy resource center, instead of an abortion clinic, I believe the whole story would have changed.

"When Karen discovered she was pregnant a second time, Miriam said, 'I don't remember feeling a lot of emotion. I took her to the abortion clinic. We knew what the drill was. I remember the third abortion the least but I do remember the last one, the fourth. I told Karen I couldn't be a party to this anymore. I guess I was starting to realize this was not the right thing to do.'

"After the last abortion, Karen said she was living dangerously, wanting to die but afraid to kill herself. Soon after, she found Jesus and her healing journey began. She started to volunteer at a pregnancy resource center and was required to go through an abortion-recovery program.

"'I had no idea all that was left in me, but for the first time I was able to grieve the loss of my four children.' She named the children David, Joseph, Sarah, and Steven—they were the only children she would ever conceive—and held a memorial service at her home that was attended by her whole fam-

ily. That memorial service began Miriam's journey in coming to terms with the loss of four grandchildren. 'I didn't fully realize the impact of what had happened,' she said, 'but that was an awakening to me.'

"Around Christmas, as she looked at the stockings hanging in her home for her other grandchildren she realized, 'there were no stockings for those four.' So she made four stockings for those lost babies. Sewing those stockings 'was a time for me to weep and heal, and realize the impact of what happened.'

"She also started volunteering at a pregnancy resource center and began facilitating an abortion-recovery program with Karen. They now run their own abortion-recovery ministry called Deeper Still, in Fallbrook, California (www.deeperstillfallbrook.org).

"'God had taken something that was dark and turned it into such a beautiful relationship with my daughter,' Miriam said. 'God has blessed us. We have this sweet time together to help other women, men, and grandparents mourning the loss of their grandchildren. With abortion, we've hurt our whole society. It's something we need to address.'"

How poignant that Miriam made those Christmas stockings for her grandchildren lost to abortion. Abortion dehumanizes babies, and in the act of making something so tangible and familiar as Christmas stockings, she restored humanity and dignity to those children. And she reached a deeper level of healing. This is a great example of how healing can overcome the shockwaves of pain.

Now let's take a look at a mother who forced her daughter to have an abortion she didn't want.

Kelly Lang's story:

"*I was 17. I had just graduated from high school and was looking forward to college and my 18th birthday. It was a summer to remember—or so I thought—one filled with dreams and hope. But little did I know that soon my life would take a dramatic turn for the worse. For it was later that summer that I had an abortion—an event that devastated me and left me with a bitterness that would haunt me for decades to come.*

"*My memory of that event begins on a hot, muggy, June afternoon, as my sister and I were taking a walk around our neighborhood. I shared with her my fear that I might be pregnant and my concerns as to how our mother might react if and when she found out. Later that day, my sister drove me to a clinic in Wichita for a pregnancy test. My sister warned me to prepare myself for trouble when I finally told my mom.*

"*As my sister had predicted, my mother did not receive the news well—advising me to have an abortion, in part because the love of my life was older than me and I was technically still a minor, being a few weeks shy of eighteen. My mother quickly decided on a course of action. She informed me that I would in fact be going to college, in spite of my pregnancy. She contacted the Wichita clinic and got them to schedule an abortion for me for the next week. She told me that I was not to see my boyfriend until after the procedure was completed. She further informed me that she would drive me to the clinic. After returning home, she would call my boyfriend and tell him to drive to Wichita to bring me home.*

"*I was to pay half of the fee and he was to pay the other half. If I did not agree to her demands, she would have him prosecuted for statutory rape.*

"Over the next few days, my mother spent more time with me than at any other time in my life. Sadly, this was not because she wanted to share my few moments of pregnancy with me. Rather it stemmed from a fear that if I were to spend time with my boyfriend, we would find a way to not have the abortion.

"No amount of tears changed my mother's mind. She was determined—and that was that. To make matters worse, as we were leaving town headed for the clinic, I saw the father of my child. The memory of seeing him like that has burned a scar on my heart that still bleeds tears.

"The trip to the clinic was filled with pleading and begging. But no amount of pleading touched my mother's heart. Arriving at the clinic, my mother signed the paperwork handed to her. As we waited for my name to be called, I tried one last time to sway her, pleading with her, 'Please mom! Please don't do this.'

"The nightmare continued as my name was called and I was led to a small office halfway down a long hallway. The lady behind the desk asked me if I had any questions. As the last word left her mouth, I was on my feet, running down the hallway, throwing open the double waiting room doors – still pleading and begging for mercy. I fell to my knees sobbing. It was then that I felt my arms being pulled upward and I was dragged to a room where my baby was sucked away.

"I lived with the consequences of this nightmare for the next thirty years—constantly waking up to the pain, the void, the anger, the depression, the loneliness, and the self-destructive impulses I experienced every day. I was convinced that everything that ever went wrong in my life was a punishment for having aborted my baby."

More than thirty years elapsed and Kelly had been through healing at Rachel's Vineyard before she finally confronted her mother about that horrific day.

"Her comment to me was that she really didn't remember. It was one of the most traumatic experiences of my life, and my mom said she didn't even remember it."

Kelly and her mom, who died on January 22, 2015 (the 42nd anniversary of *Roe v. Wade*), never fully reconciled over the abortion but Kelly said they came close a few years ago when she was asked to write her abortion story for a magazine. As she wrote, she found herself staring at a purple glass picture frame that she had purchased but never found the right photo for.

"I realized there would never be a picture there. That was where the picture of my child should have been."

At Kelly's mother's house, there was also an empty picture frame. A picture of Kelly's son had filled the frame, but he went through a period of self-consciousness and removed his photo.

"That empty frame sat on my shelf in her house for four years. I came to see that it represented the grandchild she forced me to abort, my daughter Rachel Charlotte."

Although she has been speaking openly about her abortion for many years, Kelly never spoke about her mother's role in it until after her death.

"She was still my mom. She was blind to the truth of abortion."

At the first of the nationwide protests outside Planned Parenthood in August 2015, Kelly told her whole story and was then interviewed by Fox News.

"When I realized the story was out, I cried. It was like I exposed her but I didn't dishonor her."

The day after her mom died, a priest assured Kelly that her mom and her daughter would now be able to have their own relationship in heaven, and that brings Kelly comfort and closure.

Kelly's mom never acknowledged the death of her grandchild but isn't it interesting that both she and Kelly kept empty picture frames on a shelf in their homes. Kelly believes that was her mom's attempt to silently acknowledge this grandchild. But now think of all the grandparents who have lost grandchildren to abortion and have never been able to acknowledge the existence of these children. Our society has lost generations of children to abortion. The shockwaves of abortion are impacting grandparents, but many of them are too numb to feel its impact.

Grandparents can understand that their daughter's abortion was a deeply painful experience for her, but they rarely consider their own personal need to grieve the loss of their grandchild. But grandparents, after they grieve and heal, can encourage reconciliation and healing for the entire family.

Chapter Seven

Missing from the Family Portrait

Typically, when a woman has an abortion she isn't thinking about the impact of the abortion on children she might have later on in life or already has. But research by Canadian psychiatrist Dr. Philip Ney convincingly shows that siblings are impacted by their mother's abortion.

Sibling survivors constitute one of ten distinct groups of "abortion survivors." They may feel a profound sense of emptiness, anxiety, and guilt and have complicated relationships with their parents.

Sibling survivors struggle to understand their value as a human being in light of their siblings' lives discarded through abortion. This is an extremely important and rarely discussed example of the collateral damage from the abortion earthquake. Dr. Ney reflects on his experience with his patients who have experienced abortion:

"Observations of psychiatric patients led me to believe that some people were deeply affected by surviving when someone near and dear to them, usually a sibling, died from a pregnancy loss. The symptoms appeared to be most pronounced if the loss was as a result of abortion. Statistically analyzed data showed the most frequent and intense symptom was feeling that they did not deserve to be alive. That was closely correlated to a sense of impending doom, guilt about surviving, pessimism

about the future, not trusting caregivers, and other existential symptoms that form a fairly closely circumscribed syndrome. These were significantly associated with recurrent depression, intense obsessions, suicidal risk taking, and frequent hospitalizations."

Now let's hear from some of the sibling survivors.

Kim shared her story:

"My mom was 17 years old when she got pregnant with me. Her boyfriend was much older. Even though abortions were illegal at the time, people knew where they could go to get them. My mom was scared and she wanted an abortion. Her boyfriend talked her out of it and even asked her to marry him. I was born. My parents got divorced a few years later. My mom was married three times by the time she was 24 years old.

"I liked her third husband very much. He was like a dad to me. We were poor but I didn't know we were poor for many years. I was an 'only child.' I always wanted a brother or sister. I used to talk about it and dream about having a brother or sister. One day, my mom and step-dad were in the car when I got out of school. That was odd; I usually walked home. I was happy to have a ride home. I think I was about 7 years old. I asked why they were there and where we were going. My mom said, 'I have a baby in my tummy.' I was so excited that I was jumping in the car. In the next breath, my mom told me that we couldn't afford to keep the baby. My heart sank—what did that mean? Would the baby have to live somewhere else? To my horror, this is how I first learned about abortion. My mom said she had an appointment with 'the doctor' so he could take the baby out of her tummy. I cried and felt a pain that I cannot even explain. I actually felt sick. I begged her not to go. In a minute, my dream of having a brother or sister

was a reality and in the next minute, it was a night-mare! How could I possibly love this baby so much when I just found out about him or her? I yearned for this baby. We drove to the 'doctor's office' and I sat in the car with my step-dad while my mom went in and had an abortion.

"By this time, abortion was legal. Maybe that helped my mom make her decision. It can't be that bad if it is legal, right? WRONG! She regretted that abortion for the rest of her life! Every time she saw a child who would have been the same age as the baby she aborted, she started to cry. Some nights, I would wake up to her crying. Sometimes, she would be curled-up in a ball rocking herself on the floor. She was almost always in the dark. She never got over it. As for my step-dad, he never got to have a child. My mom divorced him and remarried. My mom never had another child. So, I am an only child—or am I?

"I believe God had a plan for that baby and I wonder what he or she would have been like. I am married to a wonderful man and we have three beautiful sons. To this day, my mother's abortion affects us all. My husband had two sisters but his youngest sister died of Hodgkin's disease when she was only 27 years old. His other sister has one son. Since I have no earthly siblings, my boys have just one cousin. How different would their lives be if that baby had lived? How many cousins would my boys have?

"I am grateful that my father talked my mom out of aborting me. To think, I was once a 'CHOICE.' My three sons would not have been born and all of the children that they will have would not have been born. I love genealogy and in going back just 8 or 10 generations I found more than 1,000 relatives. When one baby is killed, how many lives are impacted? Thousands!"

In Kim's case not only did she long for a baby brother or sister but her trauma was even deeper because her mother forced her to be present at the abortion. Her mother left her in the car with her stepfather, so why she had to tell a seven-year-old child about her abortion, we will never know, but clearly this has impacted Kim. Notice also the generational impact from this abortion— the shockwaves at work.

Magaly Llaguno shared:

"God protected me from having an abortion but He gave me an awareness of the value of life and I did suffer because of abortion.

"When I was a teenager, my mother asked me to go with her to an abortion clinic. This was in Cuba where abortion was very, very common even though abortion on-demand was not legal at that time. I begged my mother not to abort that child. I did everything I could. I said to her, 'I will raise it, mom!' And I was only a teenager. 'I will raise it; I will take care of it for you.' And she smiled and she said, 'What would people think? Look how old you are already.'

"And I remember sitting in that clinic, inside, and waiting for her to finish and just wondering what more I could've done. I was not a Christian. I didn't really know how bad abortion was. In my heart I felt that it was something bad, but I never really knew until I saw the pictures of an abortion. And I never really knew for many years how much anger I had inside of me against my mother. It took years. We were never close after that.

"I attempted suicide shortly after that. And most of my life, I felt that I really had to be the best at everything, because I really had to make it worth-while that she allowed me to be born. I later found out that she had aborted seven children. And every

time we sat at the dinner table, I would think about those who were not there. There's tremendous pain when you're a sibling and your mother aborts. And I'm sure there are many people out there who are feeling this pain.

"I got involved in the pro-life movement and I have been in it for over thirty years. And when I first saw the abortion pictures, an internal voice said to me, 'That's what your brother looked like when he was aborted.' I wrote a letter to my brother I have not met, who I will meet in heaven.

"Brothers and sisters, abortion hurts. For years I went through post-abortion syndrome. I didn't know that you could go through post-abortion syndrome if you haven't had an abortion yourself, but I did.

"My mother realized what she had done, so many years later, when she saw one of my presentations. It was a great pain for me to have her present. I never told her how bad it was, but she came to one of my presentations and she saw what abortion is and she said, 'If only I had known! I love all my children. If only someone had told me. If only I had known.' Till the day she died, she regretted her abortions."

Both Kim and Magaly, who died in 2013, not only had the trauma of losing a sibling to abortion but in both cases they were taken to the abortion clinic with their mothers. They knew their mothers were coming home without their baby brother or sister, which was extremely damaging to both of them. It wasn't until many years later that Magaly was able to recognize the shockwaves in her own life and then reconcile with her mother. Her mother, also acknowledging the shockwaves, was able to apologize for the death of these babies and speak of her deep regret.

Whitney wrote:

"I grew up in a Christian home with two siblings. I often told my mom that I wished she would have had more children, because I wanted more siblings. When I was 12 years old, my mom was crying one Mother's Day (as she did every year), and we asked her what was wrong. She told us that she had gotten pregnant as a teenager and when she wouldn't abort, her fiancé skipped town to join the military and her father (my Grandaddy) sent her away to an unwed mother's home, where she was forced to give the baby up for adoption. That was my older brother, John, who we later found and reunited with. So I had my wish, another brother out there for me and I couldn't wait to find him. But then one night, I had a very remarkable dream. I was 22 years old and dreamt I was carrying on a conversation with a woman. This woman looked like she belonged in Heaven. She had no wings and was not an angel, but she had a glow about her and I know it sounds cliché; but she was wearing a white robe. She looked to be in her early thirties, had blondish hair, looked quite a lot like my mom and even reminded me of her, too. I had a burning knowledge in the dream that I absolutely had to find out this woman's name, that for some reason her name was of vital importance. This preoccupation may be the reason I don't remember anything of our conversation, but as she turned to leave, I yelled out, 'What is your name?' The woman turned around rather slowly and with a somewhat solemn tone said 'Sarah.' I remember thinking, 'That's it? Why was that so important? It's a very ordinary name.'

"But a couple weeks passed and the dream stayed with me; it felt different than any dream I had had before. So one day, as I visited mom, I began to tell her about this dream. She only half paid attention because she was working on some

craft at the time, but I still relayed all the detail and weird nature of the dream. When I told her that I knew somehow that it was so important that I find out the young woman's name, Mom said, 'So, what was her name?' I responded, 'Sarah' and my mom gasped, as she immediately turned pale. Then everything was instantly weird and I knew something was going on. My mother was the most pro-life person I knew, so you can imagine how I felt when she said, 'There's something I never told you.'

"She told me she got pregnant one year after giving my half-brother John up for adoption. Mom said the pain of giving up a baby was so great, that she decided to abort this new child. My head was reeling at this revelation. It was like mom had lived a secret life and this was difficult to swallow because my mom is the most open-book person you could meet. She said that after the abortion, her parents never spoke of it again and she never shared it with anyone; like it never happened. She became a Christian some time later and told me she realized that abortion was murder and a sin. She asked the Lord's forgiveness and He forgave, as He always does. But she never mentioned this again until she went on a week-long Christian women's conference where she shared the story.

"One of the women in her group told mom that she had known many women who had lost their babies through miscarriage or abortion and that it was actually a very healing step to name the baby. She explained that all babies go to Heaven because they are real people, and it helps the grieving process to realize that and name the baby. She then asked mom if the doctors had told her whether the baby was a boy or a girl and my mom said that they had not, but she always somehow knew in her heart that her baby had been a girl. So mom thought about it and decided to name her Sarah!

My head was exploding and mom was suddenly very interested in re-hearing all the details of the dream. Mom asked how old Sarah looked and I guessed about thirty-two, and mom told me that is exactly how old she would have been if allowed to live here on Earth. I told her that Sarah's hair was cut in the same manner as mom's had been when she was in her early thirties, except that it was noticeably more blonde (mom and I have medium brown hair). My mom told me that Sarah's father had naturally blonde hair!

"I wish I had known when I had the dream that Sarah was my sister. I would have given her such a great big hug."

Whitney, while not knowing any information about this aborted sibling, had a dream that was pretty accurate according to the details her mother later provided. Once again we see this strong longing for having this sibling in her life and the very deep void she felt by the death of a child she never met.

Now let's hear from Daniel, the son of David from San Antonio who we heard from earlier.

"I have heard others' pro-life testimonies of their struggle and loss, but the testimony that impacts me the most is my dad's. For years, I wondered, if my father is David Sr., why my brother David is not David Jr. Now I understand that David Junior never made it into this world.

"My dad told us his story after my brother, David II, asked him if he ever had an abortion. My dad bravely sat us down at the dinner table, all three of us, his children, and opened up his life story. He held nothing back, explaining the struggles of his relationship with my mom, the affair he had, and the destruction he brought upon himself and his child, my brother, with this other woman. He courageously told us and the world his testimony

at the March for Life a few years ago. He is my
role model, my inspiration, but most of all he's my
father and I love him."

Daniel's knowledge of his aborted siblings led him to
become very active in the pro-life movement. He currently heads up the pro-life group on his college campus
and he does so in memory of his aborted sibling.

Nick shared:

"When I was 12 years old and in seventh grade, I
began praying outside abortion mills, even though
at that time I didn't have a clear picture of what
abortion truly was or how it affected the people
involved. It wasn't until my freshman year that I
truly knew what I was doing in front of that clinic.

"Three months before I was scheduled to attend
the March for Life in D.C., my parents went away
for a weekend. But before they should have been
home, my brother drove my sister and me to a con-
vent. We were greeted by a priest who told us he
would bring us to our parents. We joined my parents in an office and a woman told us we were at
a Rachel's Vineyard retreat for women and others
who have been hurt by abortion.

"My mother then told us she had had two abortions and that she and my father were attending
this retreat to help deal with their grief and guilt,
and they wanted us to be with them for the final
Mass, when prayers were offered up to the babies
who were aborted.

"Attending that Mass with my family and surrounded by other women who had abortions and
truly regretted it gave me valuable perspective and
an even better reason to believe what I do about
abortion. I was no longer going to the March for
Life just for the chance to go to D.C., but because
I had people at home and in my family who I had

to fight for, not just my mom, but the brother and sister I lost."

Nick was told about the loss of his sibling in a very safe environment. At a Rachel's Vineyard retreat where women and men come for a weekend to address their abortion loss, his parents had the insight to bring him and his other siblings to be told about their aborted sibling. A counselor and a priest provided additional support. In January 2015, Nick spoke at the Silent No More Awareness Campaign gathering in Washington, D.C. about mourning his aborted sibling.

Also at the 2015 March for Life, Maddie read a letter she had written to her three aborted siblings:

Dear John Michael, George Steven, and Mary Elizabeth,

"Even though I never had a chance to introduce myself to you as your younger sister, I miss you and love you very much. I'm sorry you never got the chance to experience having Christmas with the family, school dances, being able to see all of God's beautiful creations, and going to church as a family. I wish you were all here today just so I can share memories. Although I haven't had the chance to meet you yet, I'm looking forward to the day I greet you in heaven.

"I knew my mother was young, afraid, and confused. At her first abortion she was led to believe that this was the best thing for her to do. Afterwards, she was just left with an overwhelming sadness and emotional distress, which led to drugs, alcohol, and deep depression. During the dark time of my mother's life, she had two more abortions. My mother told me about my siblings when I was 14. After church on Mother's Day, my mom took me to the church garden and I sat down on the bench, she put her arm around me, and said, 'Madeline, there's something I need to tell you.'

"*She proceeded to tell me about her three abortions and she looked up at her, as I looked up with her, I can see her eyes water and knew she was wounded from her past. I did not say much in my response but just a simple, 'I love you, you're a wonderful mom, and I forgive you.' When reflecting on my mother's story, I feel abortion should be abolished.*

"*I made the decision to become active in the pro-life movement to educate my generation and share the truth about abortion. I stand here today in honor of you my siblings, John Michael, George Steven, and Mary Elizabeth. For you, I will always be silent no more.*"

Also at the 2015 March for Life, Kelli read a letter she wrote to her aborted sister.

Dear Mary Margaret,

"*I have known about you now for 10 years, and I still tear up every time I think of you. You would have celebrated your 39th birthday this year, my little sister. Would you have been the one sibling who would live near me, raising our families together? Would you have been the one to give my kids the joy of growing up with cousins to share their childhood? I mourn the loss of knowing you, my sister, and also the loss of possible nieces and nephews, a lifelong friendship, and the hole that is at every family gathering without you. Mary Margaret, you are loved and missed. Your sister, Kelli.*"

Kelli also shared her story:

"*My mom was single and already had a 5-year-old daughter at age 22. She was embarrassed by another pregnancy and, at the time, thought of the pregnancy as just a clump of cells.*

"*Fast forward 28 years and, in 2004, she felt very different about her baby. She went to post-abor-*

tion counseling, told her family, and now knows God's forgiveness.

"Knowing I was pro-life, she was worried that I would hate her for the abortion, but for me it was confirmation that it isn't something you just 'get over.' My mom, who defended abortion 'choice' for years and buried her feelings of guilt and regret, couldn't live with the secret any longer. She is now pro-life and has spoken about her experience at gatherings in her community.

"Frankly, I have been surprised at how much this news hurt and for how long because I would never have expected to miss someone so much who I never even knew. It has made me determined to keep her memory alive, helping others understand how much this is not just one woman's choice, but that it affects so many others for a lifetime."

In all these stories, we see how the parent's abortion caused their children to live with the shockwaves of the parent's choice.

It is essential to consider the impact abortion has on young people who, even if they are not sibling survivors, are survivors nevertheless. Anyone who was in the womb after January 22, 1973 could have become an abortion statistic.

Abortion survivors live on shaky ground. "If my mother could have aborted me, what is my life worth," they may wonder. These individuals live with a sense of worthlessness and a feeling of impending doom. They suffer existential anxiety and survivor guilt.

They are "wanted" rather than "welcomed." When one is "wanted," he or she is expected to meet the needs or demands of another. When one is "welcomed," on the other hand, his or her value is acknowledged despite others' reactions or attitudes. One abortion survivor wrote, "My parents always said they had wanted me.

I often wonder what would have happened if they had not wanted me? I feel I must stay wanted. Being wanted means existing."

Another wrote, "I had no right to exist. I am still a child trying to find a place in this world. . .wandering around, carrying the weight of something on my shoulders. I had so many unanswered questions which I could not ask because nobody would answer and besides which I could not even formulate them. All my life I have been running, running away from death, no, from something worse than death."

Whether an abortion survivor or a sibling survivor, these people are all part of the wider circle of victims impacted by abortion.

Chapter Eight

Missing from the Family Tree

We saw in the last chapter how abortion impacts the sibling survivors. In this chapter we will take a closer look at abortion's impact on family life. Secrets surrounding the abortion can foster mistrust between family members, and prevent those hurting from seeking healing.

Abortion can fracture family relationships and, at the very least, it is that very large elephant in the room no one can acknowledge. Yet the symptoms continue to be expressed by a grandmother's sleep disturbance, a grandfather's need for anxiety medication, a daughter struggling with addiction, or a son with anger issues and affairs plaguing his marriage.

When parents are weakened emotionally, spiritually, and relationally, how are the children impacted? When we look across our nation and see the epidemic of single-parent families, failed marriages, and over-medicated children in problem schools, we have to factor in the abortion connection as a contributor.

Acknowledging abortion loss can provide an avenue for deep emotional healing that can serve as the framework to build on and address other important issues that will strengthen families. Encouraging a family to heal benefits society as a whole.

Now let's look at some families and how abortion has impacted their lives.

Irene from California shared:

"*Several tragic events led up to the death of my beloved daughter, Leonor Bridgette Beltran. This is a tragedy no woman should ever have to endure, but countless women do.*

"*My husband and I met in 8th grade and became teenage sweethearts two years later. When I was 16, I gave birth to our first daughter and her five sisters soon followed. The next several years proved to be the struggle of our lives. I was 22 years old and my husband was 24. We had six daughters age 5 and under and a mortgage to pay. He worked full-time; I worked part-time, and went to school full-time. That was the beginning of the destruction of my family. I was extremely busy and my absence placed an extra burden on my husband. Our romantic evenings of laughing, cuddling, having fun together turned into arguing over the simplest of things. Arguing led to blaming and resenting each other. My husband and I separated, and my children were left with no father at home.*

"*I was confused and in despair when I became pregnant with another man's baby during my separation from my husband. We later reconciled when I was four months pregnant and my husband planned to raise the baby. The biological father did not agree with that scenario and refused to sign any adoption papers. I would talk to the daughter in my womb and tell her 'mama is going to make it all better.' I would rub my stomach at night when no one watched and say 'I love you darling.' I was so desperate to have my family back together. I was eager for my six daughters to be happy again. I love them dearly and with my warped, godless, thinking at the time, I was willing to make the ultimate sacrifice for them: Legally kill their sister, so they could have a happy family again with no reminder of the dreadful past. This was the worst thing I could have done.*

"I was 26 weeks pregnant with my daughter when I ended the life of my own child for the sake of convenience. I was shocked when I felt my child kick and punch as the abortionist administered the drug in my belly. I was inconsolable the entire time at the clinic and didn't have the strength to engage even in simple conversation with the staff. It was difficult to comprehend anything around me. I went to the labor and delivery department at a local hospital immediately two hours after they administered the lethal dose of poison to my child. I arrived at the hospital hoping doctors could save my daughter, but there was nothing they could do. The affects of the poison were irreversible. I was told the healthy beating heart I heard over the monitor would soon be stilled forever.

"The next day, after several hours in labor, I delivered an angel named Leonor Bridgette. I stroked her face and repeatedly asked her for forgiveness. My husband and I, along with my parents and other family members, were able to cradle her in our arms and spend the last moments with her before the nurse walked her small, helpless, now cold and lifeless body out of the room. My family and the biological father's family were left with the daunting task of planning her funeral. That moment I made a commitment to devote my life to protect the sanctity of life and help minimize or eliminate the victims of abortion.

"I am compelled to tell 'Leonor's Story' to protect America's children and their mothers, fathers, and siblings from the choice that I made. Leonor's death caused so much grief to so many people. It was heart-wrenching to see my daughters weep when I told them that the same mother they knew, the one who was so over-protective of them, the same mother who fed them, nurtured them, and played with them, was the same mother who ended the life of their sister.

"I recently told my 7-year-old son that I am the reason we visit his sister at the cemetery. I've hurt so many people because of the decision I've made. I've robbed my seven children of a sister they could have grown up with. I've robbed three sets of grandparents of a granddaughter; I've wiped out future generations because I destroyed the life of my daughter and her future children and their children.

"I attended 'Save One' 12-week Bible study after abortion healing program in San Bernardino, CA to help me cope and heal from the horrific memories after I ended the life of my daughter. Throughout these sessions I experienced God's love and mercy. I was finally able to give up my deeply entrenched shame and guilt. I was finally able to share my secret with other women who had similar stories. I was able to unwrap all the layers of guilt, shame, and self-hate that I carried deep within me. I received deep healing week after week and now I am compelled to speak out against the lies and destruction of abortion."

Irene's abortion didn't only impact her, her baby, and her husband and the father of the baby. The ripple effect of that abortion extended to her children who lost their sibling, the grandparents who lost a grandchild, and to the aunts, uncles, and cousins. Today Irene and her family give witness to their regret of that abortion and speak out publicly for the Silent No More Awareness Campaign. It is their hope to change hearts and minds on this issue so that people will come to understand the devastation that an abortion decision brings to an entire family and the impact it has on future generations.

Now let's take a look at the Raymond family's experience.

Chuck and Linda Raymond are Silent No More regional coordinators in St. Louis and they are very active in speaking out about the Shockwaves of abortion. Before they began to speak out, they had to tell their children and their extended family about the abortion they had as teenagers. Both Chuck's parents and Linda's parents insisted on an abortion because Chuck would have lost his appointment to West Point if they had given birth to their first child.

Even though they eventually married and had two more children, both of them suffered from the abortion. After they went through healing at a Rachel's Vineyard Retreat and decided to become active in the pro-life movement, they chose a time when both of their children were home from school for Christmas to tell them about the sibling they never knew. This was about 11 years ago.

Linda told their son Charlie by herself, while Chuck was on a business trip. Charlie was in his second year of seminary at the time.

"Charlie and I were cleaning up the kitchen and I thought to myself, 'tonight's the night,' Linda recalled. I told him the whole story, and his reaction was one of love and compassion and forgiveness. We just cried and cried and cried. When we were finished talking, he went to pray at an adoration chapel."

Later in the week, when Chuck was home, they both spoke to their daughter Michelle. She had a very different reaction.

"She had three or four more days left of her break but she left the house and went back to school. She was devastated and said she felt as if her whole life was a lie. We didn't hear from her for several more months. Finally, when it was parents' weekend at her school, Chuck drove up to see that she was OK. Chuck felt this eerie sense that we had lost her. He went to some of the parents' events and he saw her there but they didn't speak. By the end of the

weekend, she called him and asked to talk. They took a long walk all over campus and talked and talked and talked."

Linda isn't sure if Michelle ever discussed the loss of their sibling with her brother but the family has been restored to its close and supportive relationship. Charlie left seminary and both he and his sister are now married with children of their own. Michelle never mentions her missing sibling, but Charlie once said to Chuck that "I should have an older brother here helping me out." That shows that he does feel the loss of his brother on some level.

Telling their children was the first hurdle for Chuck and Linda, who felt they still had to tell their nieces and nephews. They told each one individually and were mostly met with sympathy and compassion. "We wanted to reassure each one of them and try to prevent the shockwave from traveling any further in our own family."

Discussing the abortion with their parents has proved more difficult. Chuck's mom died the same year as the abortion. Before she died, she let Chuck know that she regretted pushing the couple into the abortion. Many years later, Chuck's father told him that he also regretted having advocated for the abortion.

Linda's dad is aware that the couple is very public about their abortion story. Her father mentions their activism sometimes, but Linda has yet to have the conversation with her mother that they both need to have. Linda's mom was angry and ashamed when her daughter revealed the pregnancy. After the abortion, her mother warned her, "Don't you ever tell anybody what we did." But Linda learned many years later that her mother had told Linda's siblings and her aunts and uncles. That's another topic that still hasn't been broached.

"My mom is in a nursing home and I really want to talk to her about the abortion before she passes away,"

Linda said. "I want her to have reconciliation with the Lord, and I just want to hear what she has to say."

In the Raymond's story you will notice their daughter Michelle had an adverse reaction to the news that she lost a sibling to abortion. She said she felt like her whole life was a lie. Obviously, Michelle was shocked at the news of the sibling missing from their family portrait but her reaction to the shockwaves of abortion impacting her family goes much deeper.

Dr. Ney has studied this issue. He has seen many children who have a sense of a missing sibling.

One such case he mentions is about a mother who brought her 6-year-old child to see Dr. Ney for a bed-wetting problem. He interviewed the mother and while doing so his assistant had the child in another room and asked the child to draw a picture of his family. The child drew a picture with the mother, father, and two siblings. When Dr. Ney saw the drawing he asked the mother about all her pregnancies. It turns out the mother had two abortions. This was something that the child did not know about and yet had a sense that someone was missing from the family portrait. This family continued in counseling and had a good outcome once the truth was spoken of and healing began.

For the Raymond family, once the subject was spoken about honestly, the door to healing opened up. Chuck and Linda continue to speak publicly about their regret of their abortion and the healing they have found to encourage others to seek healing.

Catherine from North Carolina shared:

Abortion figures prominently in Catherine's family. Between her, some of her sisters, and some of her nieces, the North Carolina family lost 10 children to abortion. Catherine wonders if the loss could be greater if any of her nephews had also been involved in abortion, something she doesn't know for sure but wonders.

Catherine's own story started when she was getting close to college graduation and had just lined up her dream job in broadcast journalism. "I realized I was pregnant and thought, 'I have to get rid of this inconvenience, and I did,'" she recalled. Her college roommate, who already had an abortion, drove her to the clinic.

Catherine had been involved with two men when she found out she was pregnant, an older married man and a young college friend she slept with just one time. Catherine says she knew it was the younger man's baby but told the older man it was his, so he would pay for the abortion.

"My behavior didn't change after that, even though I promised God. I was still drinking, taking drugs, and being promiscuous. It was a crazy environment, non-stop partying, it was the early '80s and the sex, drugs, and rock and roll culture was in full swing—even at work. A year-and-a-half later, I was pregnant again."

This time the stakes were higher because of her visibility in the community. A co-worker arranged for her to have the abortion in a doctor's office. "I remember he was an arrogant guy who drove a Rolls Royce," Catherine said. "Several months later I ran into him at a party, and he made the rudest comment to me, saying I had probably helped pay for a spoke on his tire."

When Catherine realized 30 years later how much damage the abortion caused her emotionally, she knew she needed healing, which she found, and then felt called to speak publicly, so she started with her family. The full extent of the damage abortion had done to Catherine's family began to be revealed.

Catherine's oldest sister not only considered aborting her second child—he's now a happily married 43-year-old businessman—but also took her 15-year-old daughter for an abortion. That girl is now a 45-year-old woman who never married, never had another child, and had to undergo a hysterectomy.

Another of Catherine's sisters was a rebellious soul and ran away to Haight Ashbury in San Francisco when she was 16 to join the hippies and the free love movement. This sister ended up having four abortions and was six months pregnant when she married her second husband, an alcohol and drug addict. Her two oldest daughters also had abortions. Catherine said the prevailing attitude was "it's no big deal, God's forgiven me. It's what you do when you get in trouble."

Even Catherine's 92-year-old aunt had an abortion while her husband was fighting in World War II and she had an affair that led to pregnancy. And Catherine's husband also lost one child to abortion.

"The people who are missing from my family could fill a whole room," Catherine said. "My nephews, who knows? Now, one of my fears is that my daughter will get pregnant and choose abortion. She's just like me."

After Catherine's second abortion, she became a radical feminist, which she now recognizes as an effort to validate her choices.

"Looking back on the choices I made, I didn't realize the profound emotional impact the abortions would have on my life. I buried them in the deep recesses of my soul where they stayed for the next three decades. I moved on with life, feeling bogus and unworthy, but strained forward in my motherhood, marriage, career, and community involvement.

"I became a strong pro-abortion supporter and spent many years fighting to protect women's reproductive rights. I was an outspoken advocate for choice—at times militant—with anyone who didn't agree with my opinion. I even lobbied lawmakers, hosted events for pro-choice candi-

dates and was on my way to becoming a Planned Parenthood board member when my heart dramatically changed—thank God!

"A powerful message clearly came to me that I could no longer fight against the lives of the unborn. God's grace allowed me to see clearly that life is sacred. I began regretting my abortions and attended a Rachel's Vineyard Retreat for post-abortive men and women where I finally received the tremendous healing I so desperately needed. I learned to forgive myself and give dignity to the precious lives I took. As for my sisters and other family members I hope and pray that they will someday come to terms with the impact abortion has had on our family."

As you can see, abortion sends shockwaves of pain through whole families. If you consider that we have about one million abortions annually in the United States, that translates into millions of family members impacted in some way.

In 2015 the Catholic Church held a Synod of Bishops from around the world to address the crisis in families. Here's a quote from the document that Pope Francis issued on the conclusion of this Synod.

"If the family is the sanctuary of life, the place where life is conceived and cared for, it is a horrendous contradiction when it becomes a place where life is rejected and destroyed. So great is the value of a human life, and so inalienable the right to life of an innocent child growing in the mother's womb, that no alleged right to one's own body can justify a decision to terminate that life, which is an end in itself and which can never be considered the 'property' of another human being" (Sec. 83, *The Joy of Love, Amoris Laetitia*).

Chapter Nine

Friends Don't Let Friends
Get an Abortion

Friends don't let friends drive drunk, and neither should they take a friend for an abortion. In this chapter we will explore the impact of helping a friend to have an abortion. Friends might be an accomplice in an abortion by driving to the clinic or helping to pay for the procedure. Friends who are silent about the abortion are also complicit. These friends, too, can suffer from abortion regret.

When family and friends are aware of a woman's abortion decision, but fail to help the mother find alternatives or voice their objection, or if they simply express ambivalence or say nothing in response to her decision, these reactions can lead to the death of an unborn child.

You may think people aren't really impacted by a friend's abortion but we know by the fact that many of these people seek healing programs that they, too, feel the shockwaves of that abortion.

Also in this chapter, we will explore in a deeper way the different categories of survivors that have been studied by Dr. Ney.

Let's take a look at a woman who took her friend to an abortion clinic.

Kathy from Massachusetts explains:

"During college, a friend came to me and told me she was pregnant. We sought the help of a college administrator we both trusted. She presented us with details about how and where to get an abortion. My friend looked me in the eye and asked me what I thought she should do. Both of us were 'cradle Catholics' attending a Catholic college. I knew abortion was wrong and a grave sin. So I said what our culture had brainwashed me to say: 'You should do what you think is right. I will support you.' At that instant, a voice inside of me screamed 'No!' but I didn't have the courage or the words to say what I really felt.

"I thought I was being a supportive friend. I thought the burden of this sin would be totally hers, and I was an innocent bystander just helping her do what she wanted to do. Deep down, I was even a bit angry with her for putting me in this situation. I drove her to the abortion facility three hours away. I was not permitted to go inside with her, so I had to leave her to face this horrible ordeal alone. I felt guilty and helpless. I felt weak when she needed me to be strong. I was ashamed for my lack of courage to do the right thing.

"After the abortion, I drove her back to school. We spoke briefly about what happened for the next few days. Even though we remained good friends and have seen one another over the years since graduation, we did not speak about her abortion again for 28 years!

"Eventually, I realized I was complicit in the death of this child and joined the 40 Days for Life Campaign to pray outside a local abortion clinic. I felt this was my penance.

"A few years later, I volunteered as a counselor at a local pregnancy center, and God put me on the

path to be trained as a leader in a post-abortion Bible study healing program called Surrendering the Secret. Now I have the courage and the words to care for women who suffer in silence and struggle alone to be healed and forgiven. By leading this program, I could finally be a true friend to post-abortive women, a friend I had not been to my college friend so long ago.

"Shortly after my training, I called my college friend. For the first time in 28 years, I asked her, 'How are you doing with your abortion?' I asked her if she had been healed and if she thought about her baby. I asked for her forgiveness. I apologized to her for letting her down when she needed me most.

"She kindly forgave me. I feel so much better speaking with her openly about the abortion and her baby instead of holding the secret deep down inside when I am with her. She is healed, forgiven, and spiritually connected to her son. Plus, she is happy knowing that I am 'Silent No More' and reaching out to help free other post-abortive women from their isolation and pain."

Notice that Kathy knew abortion was wrong and yet when faced with an opportunity to help her college friend, she fell back on the "I will support you in whatever you decide" rhetoric. I know from the testimonies of the women of Silent No More that kind of a response is opening the door to abortion. What Kathy's friend and so many women facing an unexpected pregnancy are looking for is assistance and hope. It's telling to see that Kathy could not forgive herself until after she was forgiven by her friend.

Colleen from Georgia told us her story:

"I was a fallen, non-practicing Catholic at the age of thirty. I was seeking God in all the wrong places. I was empty and devoid of joy, partying and

*escaping my deep emptiness in bars and in the con-
sumption and abuse of alcohol. It was during that
time that a friend of mine got pregnant. She knew
that the father would have nothing to do with
the baby, and she could not afford to be a single
mother. She made a very humble income teaching,
as did I. We were colleagues, both teachers at a
prestigious university in Massachusetts. She mat-
ter-of-factly said she would get an abortion. I don't
even know how far along she was.*

*"At the time, and I say this with utter heartache,
I did not even blink an eye. I said, 'OK, I'll drive you
there.' I don't recall why I stayed in the car. I did
not even go into the clinic with her. I remember
that afterward she walked out, got in the car, and
said she didn't feel well, that she just wanted to lie
down. So I dropped her off at her apartment. She
did not really seem like she wanted me to stay. She
wanted to rest and be alone, so I left. We never
talked about her abortion again. I recall now how
cold-hearted I was about the entire event. I treated
it, and she did as well, like she just went to the doctor to be treated for a cold or a migraine.*

*"That day haunts me. How did I become so lost
and soulless and selfish and vacant? After I met
my husband, he slowly led me back to my Catholic
faith, and I have since confessed my sin. The priest
very gently told me that in the eyes of the Church,
my sin was as grave as if I had committed abortion
myself. I never knew that. So while I know in my
heart that God has forgiven me, I still cry about
it. I have not been able to forgive myself for what I
have done."*

Colleen knows God has forgiven her, but she cannot
forgive herself. Kathy went through an abortion recovery program, learned to forgive herself and also sought
the forgiveness of her friend. Kathy has found peace and
that peace is available to Colleen as well.

Many people consider their sisters their best friends. Let's hear from Margaret from New Mexico:

"My name is Margaret and I regret my part in my sister's abortion. Twenty-five years ago, my sister came to me for advice. She was young, unmarried, tearful, and pregnant. She wanted to know what she should do. I love my sister very much, and I cared about her and her 'problem.' I wanted her to be happy. In my mind, her only option was abortion. I never considered offering to help raise her child or helping her through an adoption. I was smug, self-righteous, and convinced I was right. I did not even care much about the father. I remember telling her that if she and the father agreed that the abortion was 'for the best' then it was the right thing to do.

"I went with her to the abortion clinic. I never thought of the baby in terms of being a person. I never thought of the baby as my own niece or nephew. It never entered my mind that she would suffer the emotional effects of abortion for the rest of her life.

"For the next twenty years, I never thought about her abortion. Until recently, I have never even asked her if she was OK. I used to believe that it was a woman's choice to do what she wanted to do with her own body because it was her body and nobody's business. If asked, I would proudly say that I was pro-choice. It never occurred to me that the tiny person being nurtured in their mother's womb was not given a choice.

"During this time, I had distanced myself from the Catholic Church and never thought about the meaning of 'Thou shall not kill' or applying it to a child in the womb. When I married and had a child, my husband and I agreed to raise him Catholic

as we had been raised, so we came home to the Church. As I nurtured my relationship with God, I realized that my advice to my sister to have an abortion was wrong. I started to wonder whether her baby had been a boy or a girl. I realized that her child was my niece or my nephew. I cried. I mourned for this child that I would never meet, this child who would never be my son's older cousin. This child who was our mother and father's first grandchild.

"For years, I have struggled with the guilt and shame about my involvement in my sister's abortion. My heart has ached for this child. I ache because I never had the chance to hold this child, play with him or her, or pick them up when they fell. I never got to see this child grow up and fall in love. My son never had an older cousin who might have enriched his 'only child' life. I hurt to my very soul. I love this child so very much.

"Over the years, I have noticed that when I speak about my pro-life activities or being pro-life in general, my sister tears up. I learned to curb my words because the mere mention of the word pro-life is painful for her to hear. I care that she is in pain. I pray that one day soon she will find forgiveness and peace.

"My sister was silent for many years, telling only select friends. In preparation to write my testimony, I met with her to ask her permission to identify her in my testimony. I wanted her to know how I was feeling about my involvement and how this abortion has affected my life. I arranged this meeting knowing full well that she might reject my request. I was pleasantly surprised when she said yes. Until then, we had not really talked about the how the abortion impacted our lives. In 20 years, I have only broached the subject once through email because it was too hard to ask her face-to-face how

she felt about her abortion. As we talked about her abortion decision, she reiterated the words from so long ago that it was the best decision. She said she would not have been able to raise the child well. I could not continue the conversation because it was too painful. I truly feel and believe that I have been called to help those who suffer from the effects of abortion. I regret my advice to my sister to have an abortion."

Other Survivors

Now we will explore these additional survivor categories, identified by Dr. Ney and his wife, Dr. Marie Peeters Ney in their research.

1. Statistical survivors. These are people who survived in countries or cities where there is a statistically high probability that they would have been aborted. They come to know that the odds were definitely stacked against them. In some parts of Eastern Europe, the chances of being aborted are as high as 80 percent.

2. Wanted survivors. These are people whose parents carefully deliberated about whether or not to abort them. They may have calculated, consulted, and discussed the possibility.

We have heard stories from children who, as teenagers or even older, were told by their mothers that they should have been aborted. One of these stories comes from Alveda King, the director of Priests for Life's Civil Rights for the Unborn and a niece of the Rev. Dr. Martin Luther King, Jr. When Alveda's mother, Naomi and her husband Rev. A.D. King (MLK's brother) were pregnant with Alveda, she considered an abortion. This was before *Roe v. Wade*. Naomi decided not to abort Alveda after speaking to her pastor, Rev. Martin Luther King, Sr. Alveda grew up not knowing her mother's original plan to abort her. Many years later, after Naomi told her, Alveda began to understand some experiences she had growing up that heightened her feeling of not being wanted. For instance, from time to time her mother would yell at Alveda saying, "You are always messing things up for me." Alveda felt like she was always trying to measure up, to make her mother happy—to stop messing things up. Alveda and Naomi have spoken honestly about this to each other and now share their story so that other families can find healing and restoration the way they have.

3. Sibling survivors. These are people born into families where one or more of their siblings were aborted.

As we discussed in the previous chapter, children who are born after a sibling was aborted have a strong sense that someone is missing. Even if his or her parents never speak about the abortion, they may have a sense of a missing brother or sister. Dr. Ney said some children invent an imaginary friend to make up for the missing—and missed—sibling.

4. Threatened survivors. These are children whose parents have used abortion as a threat, even if they never considered it during the pregnancy: "You wretched, ungrateful child...I should have aborted you!"

5. Disabled survivors. These are people who, because of developmental defects or other circumstances, would usually be aborted. In fact, they often wonder whether their parents would have aborted them had they known about the defects.

6. Chance survivors. These are children who would have been aborted if the mother had been able to obtain the abortion. The abortion was prevented by a lack of money, time, permission, availability, etc.

7. Ambivalent survivors. These are children of parents who could not make up their minds about the abortion and delayed until it was too late. They are often

caught up in their parents' continuing ambivalence, and wonder whether they can still be terminated.

8. Twin survivors. These are people whose twin was aborted. Twins communicate, touch, and even caress each other in the womb. The loss of the twin by abortion is deeply felt and can even cause the survivor to consider suicide later in life.

Here's a story of a twin survivor.

Sarah's mother, Betty, tried to abort Sarah in Los Angeles. At the time, Betty did not know she was pregnant with twins. One baby was aborted, but miraculously, Sarah survived. Sarah has forgiven her mother—and for five years they traveled the world speaking together about the pain and suffering caused by abortion. This is Sarah's story:

"My mother decided to have an abortion. At the time, she was pregnant with twins, but nobody knew this, not even her doctor. My tiny brother and I were both growing in her womb, until that dreadful day. Before the abortion, we were both alive. Moments later, I was alone.

"It's frightening to think I was almost aborted when my mom had a D&C abortion. Somehow, miraculously, I survived! My twin brother wasn't so lucky. Andrew was aborted and we lost him forever.

"Several weeks later, my mother was shocked to feel me kicking in her womb. She already had five children and she knew what it felt like when a baby kicked in the womb. She instantly knew that somehow she was still pregnant. She went back to the doctor and told him she was still pregnant—that she had made a big mistake and that she wanted to keep this baby.

"To this day, my mother deeply regrets that abortion. I know the pain is unbearable for her at

times when she looks at me and knows she aborted my twin brother.

"After surviving the abortion, I was born with bilateral, congenital dislocated hips and many other physical handicaps. Nine days after I was born, I was taken to an orthopedic surgeon who applied a cast to each of my tiny legs. My mom would remove these casts with pliers every Monday morning and take me to the doctor to have new casts put on.

"At six weeks I was put into my first body cast. Many surgeries and body casts followed over the next few years. Today, I thank God I survived the abortion, but the pain continues for everyone in my family."

9. Attempted murder survivors. These are people who survived an actual abortion attempt. In addition to the physical harm, they suffer intense psychological struggles, nightmares, confused identities, and a fear of doctors.

Melissa Ohden survived an abortion. This is her testimony to the House Judiciary Committee in September, 2015:

"I should have been just another statistic. I am the survivor of a failed saline infusion abortion— the exact wording in my records reads—'a saline infusion for an abortion was done but was unsuccessful.'

"It has taken years to unravel the secrets surrounding my survival, to have contact with my biological family and medical professionals that cared for me, and although there are still unanswered questions, what I do know is that my life was intended to be ended by an abortion, and even after I survived, my life was in jeopardy.

"You wouldn't know it by looking at me today, but in August of 1977, I survived a failed saline infusion abortion. A saline infusion abortion involves injecting a toxic salt solution into the amniotic fluid surrounding the preborn child. The intent of that salt solution is to scald the child to death, from the outside in.

"For days, I soaked in that toxic salt solution, and on the fifth day of the procedure, my biological mother, a 19-year-old college student, delivered me, after her labor was induced. I should have been delivered dead, as a successful abortion.

"In 2013, I learned through contact with my biological mother's family that not only was this abortion forced upon her against her will, but also that it was my maternal grandmother, a nurse, who delivered me in this final step of the abortion procedure at St. Luke's Hospital in Sioux City, Iowa.

"Unfortunately, I also learned that when my grandmother realized that the abortion had not succeeded in ending my life, she demanded that I be left to die.

"I may never know how, exactly, two nurses who were on staff that day (one of whom has had part of her story passed down to my adoptive family) found out about me, but what I do know is that their willingness to fight for medical care to be provided to me saved my life.

"I know where children like me were left to die at St. Luke's Hospital—in a utility closet. In 2014, I met a nurse who assisted in a saline infusion abortion there in 1976, and delivered a living baby boy. After he was delivered alive, she followed her superior's orders and placed him in the utility closet in a bucket of formaldehyde to be picked up later as medical waste after he died there, alone.

"*A bucket of formaldehyde in a utility closet was meant to be my fate after I wasn't scalded to death through the abortion. Yet here I am today.*

"*I weighed a little less than 3 pounds (2 pounds, 14 ounces); I suffered from jaundice, severe respiratory problems and seizures. One of the first notations in my medical records states that I looked like I was about 31 weeks gestational age when I survived.*

"*Despite the miracle of my survival, the doctor's prognosis for my life was initially very poor. My adoptive parents were told that I would suffer from multiple disabilities throughout my life. However, here I am today, perfectly healthy.*

"*What happens to children like me who live?*

"*We are your friend, your co-worker, your neighbor, and you would likely never guess just by looking at us that we survived what we did. In my work as the founder of The Abortion Survivor's Network, I have had contact with 203 other abortion survivors.*

"*As a fellow American, as a fellow human being, I deserved the same right to life, the same equal protection under the law as each and every one of you. Yet we live in a time where such protections do not exist.*"

Melissa and many other survivors continue to give testimony. You can visit *www.TheAbortion Survivors'sNetwork.com* to read more stories like hers.

10. Murdered survivors. These are children who survived an abortion for just a short period of time, and were subsequently killed by the abortion staff or left to die.

Jill Stanek was a nurse at Christ Hospital in Illinois when she discovered that babies born alive after abortion were being left to die in a utility room, where biohazardous materials and soiled linens were kept. It was her testimony before a congressional committee in 2000 that led Congress to pass the Born Alive Infant Protection Act that President George W. Bush signed into law.

Abortion survivors, as we have seen, can have many different experiences of abortion—from the sense of a missing sibling to the certainty that they themselves were targeted for termination. These survivors experience the shockwaves of abortion in intimate, personal, and emotionally devastating ways.

Chapter Ten

The Society of Centurions

An abortion doctor who takes the life of a child is deeply impacted by each and every abortion. Just like the Centurion at the Cross of Jesus, many of these doctors have dropped their surgical instruments to say, "Surely these are innocent babies and I can't continue to do this procedure." This chapter will contain testimonies of doctors and clinic workers who have left the abortion industry and sought healing and rehabilitation.

Apart from the baby who dies and the mother who experiences abortion, this is the population most intimately involved in the abortion experience. These men and women are the people who process a patient's information and accept payment for the abortion. In many abortion businesses, these workers are also asked to perform duties that only someone with medical training should be responsible for handling. Some have had to help out in the procedure room or have been asked to count the baby's body parts to ensure the abortion is complete. If they are wrong, and a body part has been left in a woman's uterus, the mother will suffer an infection that could be life threatening.

Ending the life of an unborn child often turns out to be much harder than these doctors, nurses, and clinic workers ever imagined.

Let's hear from some of them:

Dr. Beverly McMillan was a practicing ob-gyn in Lexington, KY, in 1973 when *Roe v. Wade* and *Doe v. Bolton* legalized abortion through all nine months of pregnancy.

"My partner and I decided to start offering abortion up until 12 weeks, because after that the complications increased." The following year she moved to Mississippi, with her husband and their three sons, all under 5 years old. She opened a private practice—without abortion—in January 1975, but because she didn't know anyone in Mississippi and 'women in medicine were not welcomed with open arms,' that year turned out to be 'the worst year of my life.'"

But when she started teaching part time at a university, she ended up discussing abortion with a group of physicians who wanted to bring legal abortion to Mississippi for the first time. They couldn't find a willing doctor. So in the fall of 1975, she opened the first abortion clinic in the state.

They were busy almost immediately, and she began training other physicians because business—a sideline to her private practice—was booming.

> "I started to look at my life. I had a nice house, a new car. I had three healthy boys. Everything I had wanted to achieve I had pretty well accomplished. But I was terribly depressed. I was starting to look at what I was doing."

She vividly remembers a day in 1978 when she had just finished performing a suction abortion and began to "pick through the tissue, looking for two arms, two legs, a skull, a spine and the placenta." She couldn't find all the parts so she returned to her patient "to suction and scrape some more."

A woman in her office wanted to see the parts of the baby boy who had just been suctioned out of his mother's womb, and as she was showing them, she came across a dismembered arm with a beautiful little bicep muscle. *"I had a flashback to my youngest son, who was always trying to show his brothers he could do what they did and would make a muscle.*

"A wave of sadness came over me as I realized that five minutes ago, this had been a beautiful little boy. After that, I couldn't do abortions anymore."

Dr. McMillan quit working in the abortion clinic and kept her regular OB/GYN practice, delivering babies and dealing with women's health issues. Abortion was in her past, but also remained in her heart and soul. With every abortion performed, a little piece of the doctor dies a spiritual death. To tear a child from his mother's womb, abortionists have to dehumanize that child, but in doing so they, too, have become dehumanized.

Years after she stopped doing abortions, Dr. McMillan joined the Society of Centurions and did the abortion rehabilitation program developed by Dr. Ney. An important step in the healing process is for the abortionist to try to remember how many babies they killed by abortion. Over the next several months, and in some cases years, they are asked to re-humanize these children by naming them and writing letters to each baby, apologizing for ending his or her life and asking for forgiveness. It is in doing this that they, the abortionist, begins to be re-humanized and find peace and restoration.

Here's the story of Joseph Randall from New York, who gave his witness at a "Meet The Abortion Providers Conference" hosted by the Pro-Life Action League in 1987. Dr. Randall learned how to do abortions in 1971 in New York. Abortion was legal in several states, including New York, before *Roe v. Wade* in 1973.

"When we started, abortions were done by the D&C method. There was no suction yet. This is where you dilate and actually scrape the lining of the uterus. This took, sometimes, 15 to 20 minutes, even for an eight or ten-week fetus. It was a bloody sort of thing and we didn't like doing it when we started. One doctor was Catholic so he was allowed by his faith not to do abortion, but the rest of us went along with peer pressure. We thought about it, and we felt uncomfortable, but we did it.

"Things gradually changed. New technology came along. We developed the suction procedure and things went much quicker. It wasn't as bloody and it was a little bit easier to take. In the early days, there were panels that women had to be cleared by before they had an abortion. The panels were made up of nurses, social workers, doctors, psychologists, psychiatrists and the like, and they determined if the women could have the abortion. After suction abortions became more popular, those panels dropped by the wayside. We were doing too many abortions to have the women go through this long, arduous process of evaluation. It was a gradual desensitization, so to speak.

"The media was very active early on. They were really our major influence. The media told us that abortion was legal, that it served women, that it gave them a choice, and the freedom to grow. We believed the lie that there were tens of thousands of women being maimed and killed by illegal abortion. It kind of made things feel a little bit better.

"In 1973, after I got married, Uncle Sam got me and I moved from Albany to Atlanta with the Army. I spent two years at Fort McPherson. My wife and I had two baby boys and I began working in abortion clinics. That was the newest thing. There were seven or eight of them by that time in Atlanta. The clinics offered an easy way to make money. *I could make $25 for each abortion, but we did 20 or 30 a day. I remember one day we did 62. That was my high point, you might say, or my low point. I became the medical director of a clinic in Atlanta.*

"*But something was happening to me emotionally. I could do several hours of abortions and feel nothing. I was just a good technician. I would even get a little charge out of the fact that women would occasionally thank me for doing the abortion. But for the most part, I didn't think about it much at all. But when I got divorced, I began searching for something more. Now I was a bachelor doctor in Atlanta, doing well financially. I had all the women I wanted, and all the good times. Life in the fast lane, so to speak. I really felt that I had it made, but I still had this gnawing emptiness inside.*

"*Then a Christian girl came into my life, and she had a great influence on me. When she broke up with me, she left me with two verses from Scripture: Jeremiah 1:5 and Psalm 139:13-18. I had not read the Bible for years, but these Scriptures meant something to me. She knew I did abortions and this would hopefully change my mind. When I read them, I felt as though a knife had pierced my midsection. I knew then that I was not serving women, I was killing their babies. But I didn't stop doing abortions.*

"*At the same time, D&E procedures started at the clinic. The babies are bigger, they are fully formed, and you are tearing them apart from below. I was sent to Chicago to learn this procedure. Once I started doing them, I started feeling really uncomfortable. Ultrasound came along at about the same time, and that picture of the baby on the ultrasound bothered me more than anything else.*

"*As soon as we started doing D&E abortions, we immediately lost two nurses and some other staff. I think ultrasound was the key there. We never let the women who were having abortions look at the ultrasound because we knew if they saw the baby and heard the heartbeat they wouldn't have the abortion. You wouldn't want that—no money in that.*

"*The gnawing emptiness inside me was growing deeper and I tried everything to fill it. I got active in the Lion's Club, in medical committees, in the occult and astral projection. Nothing helped. I knew in my heart that I wanted to become a good Christian, but I knew I couldn't be a Christian abortionist. What kept me on the fence for a year-and-a-half was money. I had become trapped by the money. By now, in addition to abortion, I had a gynecology practice. I didn't do obstetrics. I gave up delivering babies because abortions were my deliveries. I was a hard-hearted sort of a guy. But there was a voice inside me that said I should stop doing abortions, no matter how much money I made, no matter how much I was paying my wife in alimony. The voice said 'Do it now.' The voice said 'Trust me.'*

"*On Saturday, October 23, 1983, I did my last abortions. That evening I said no to money and yes to God. I went to church the next day and went right up to the altar and cried there with the best of them. On the way out of church, I saw a blue brochure for a crisis pregnancy center. I knew this was what I should be doing. So the next day I called up and said I was a doctor in Atlanta and had done many, many thousands of abortions and that I came to Christ the day before. Well, there was silence on the phone. Finally the man on the phone said that we should talk, and we did, and he told me that people needed to hear my story. So that is what I've been doing ever since.*"

The shockwaves of abortion are evident throughout Dr. Randall's story. He speaks of being desensitized, yet empty. He divorced and then could not maintain a relationship with a Christian woman because he was an abortionist. He dabbled in the occult and became trapped by the money to be made in abortion. It took him several years to put abortions behind him and work on healing himself.

Dr. Anthony Levatino, a medical advisor for Priests for Life, estimates he performed about 1,200 abortions before he gave it up.

"I started doing abortions in 1977 in New York State during my OB residency. I graduated in 1980 and went into private practice, first in Florida and later in New York. In five years, I performed 1,200 abortions, including 100 second-trimester saline abortions and later, D&E abortions up to 24 weeks.

"Let me tell you about saline abortions. They are horrible because you see one intact, whole baby being born, and sometimes they are alive. That was very, very frightening. With D&E abortions, we traded one kind of brutality for another. You tear the arms and legs off babies and put them in a stack on the table. Babies are never born alive after a D&E abortion. It's hard. If you have any heart at all, it affects you.

"During this time, my wife and I found out we probably would not be able to conceive a child on our own, so we began looking for a baby to adopt. We ran up against one roadblock after another trying to find a baby to adopt while I was throwing them in the garbage at the rate of nine or ten a week.

"Finally we were able to adopt a baby girl. We named her Heather. A year later, my wife gave birth to our son.

"My daughter Heather was hit by a car in front of our home when she was two months shy of her sixth birthday. She died in our arms in the ambulance on the way to the hospital. I did a few more late-term abortions after that, but it was too difficult to continue.

"When you lose your child, life is very different. Everything changes. All of a sudden, the idea of a person's life becomes very real. It is not an embryology course anymore. It's not just a couple of hundred dollars. It's the real thing. It's your child you buried. The old discomforts came back. I couldn't even think about a D&E abortion anymore. No way. I stopped doing the second-trimester abortions. Then I came to the realization that if I shouldn't be killing children in the second trimester, then I shouldn't be killing them earlier either.

"I became involved with the pro-life movement and that has helped me to heal and to find forgiveness. How do you make up for the 1,200 dead kids? You can't, not without the grace of God.

"As an abortionist, I was at the epicenter of the earthquake but since I stopped doing abortions and became involved with pro-life efforts, I can clearly see how abortion affects everyone connected with the child who dies. I regret performing abortions."

The traumatic death of his daughter Heather forced him to realize the humanity of the children he was aborting. He could not do abortions after such a huge loss. Now he speaks publicly about his change of heart.

At the March for Life in D.C. in January 2015, carrying a sign that said "I Regret Performing Abortions," Dr. Levatino marched alongside women and men of the Silent No More Awareness Campaign who were carrying signs that said "I Regret My Abortion" and "I Regret Lost Fatherhood." He gave his testimony during our annual gathering before the U.S. Supreme Court building and it was among the most powerful events I have witnessed. The women told me afterward how much it meant to hear him apologize to the mothers he had hurt.

People who work in abortion businesses also experience the shockwaves.

Nitta Whitten went to work at an abortion business in Texas owned by Curtis Boyd—who still does late-term abortions in Albuquerque—and his wife Glenna. This testimony was extracted from her talk at a "Meet the Abortion Providers" workshop.

"When I went to work for Curtis and Glenna, they made really sure that I was all in favor of abortion. What was so funny was that I lied right through my teeth. I didn't know anything about it, I really didn't. I didn't know anybody who had one; I had never seen one; I had never been around it. All I knew was the word 'abortion' and that I was a liberal person. I was very liberal, and so therefore I could work there. I told them that it wouldn't bother me and that if I got pregnant I'd probably have an abortion. That's what I told them. They believed me and they hired me.

"Several of the people I worked with were very unusual. The woman who was instrumental in hiring me, Elaine, she was on her way to quitting the clinic because she couldn't handle it anymore.

"Elaine was hooked on valium when I was there. . . . She was really, really traumatized by what she saw every day. She was traumatized by the insensitivity to not just unborn babies' lives, but to life in general. It was hard to work for Curtis and Glenna. They'll tell you that they're doing this for the woman's sake but it's a lie. They're doing it for the money.

"Money was the big deal. We made a lot of money. Curtis and Glenna lived in a very nice home and had a second home in Santa Fe, New Mexico.

"They owned expensive things and lived like rich people. They wanted to live that way and they weren't embarrassed to live that way. They made all their money on abortions. When I worked there, they did abortions up to 19 weeks, and we had babies bigger than 19 weeks (in Texas at the time, you could only go to 24 weeks), another abortionist would fly in and do our 'big' babies on Saturdays once in awhile when we could get him there.

"One of the most interesting things that happened when I worked there was that I was trained by a professional marketing director how to sell abortions over the telephone. This man came into our clinic and he took every one of our receptionists, all of the nurses, anyone who would be on the phone, and he took us through an extensive training period. We learned how to sell abortions over the telephone so that when the 'girl' called, we hooked a sale so she wouldn't go down the street and get an abortion somewhere else, and so that she wouldn't adopt out her baby, or wouldn't change her mind. We were doing it to get her money. It was for the money.

"I'm going to tell you some gory details that happened at the clinic that I remember specifically. There was a woman who came in the clinic who was forcing her daughter to have an abortion. This wasn't uncommon at all; it happened all the time. This woman forced her daughter to come in there and she was a second trimester, probably about 15 weeks. They had inserted the laminaria the day before, and she was in there and quite miserable. The poor girl was really upset and she kept going to the bathroom, and obviously there was something wrong with her physically. When she went into the bathroom the next time, all of a sudden she started screaming at the top of her lungs. 'It's a baby; it's a baby; mama, mama, mama!' She was screaming in the middle of our clinic. So I'm freaking out and try-

ing to figure out what's going on. I called Holly, her counselor, and said, Holly, she's aborted the baby in the bathroom and you need to get the doctor right now. Well, he was in a procedure and couldn't come then. None of the nurses knew what to do, so they got her back there real quick and took care of her. But I firmly believe that without the grace of God and the healing power of Jesus Christ she's going to be scarred emotionally from having seen that baby in the toilet where it landed.

"One of the things that happened as I worked at the clinic was that I became extremely depressed, extremely despondent, and basically hooked on drugs. I had done 'fun' drugs before I started working at the clinic because of peer pressure. I thought it was fun, and I enjoyed it. But when I worked there I had to take drugs to cope. I took drugs to wake up in the morning; I took speed while I was at work; and I smoked marijuana, drank lots of alcohol, and took anything else I could buy with the money that I made. This was a daily thing. I'm not only talking about weekends; I'm saying that this is the way that I coped with what I did. It was horrible to work there and there was no good in it."

It's clear from Nitta's testimony that everyone who worked in that abortion business was part of the wider circle of victims. In another part of her testimony, Nitta said that even Glenna had nightmares. Abortion touches everyone, but its impact is felt the most by those, like Nitta, at the epicenter.

Jules from Pennsylvania worked in an abortion business.

"When I learned I was pregnant at 17, I wanted to continue the pregnancy and parent my child, but I had no support from my boyfriend, my friends, or my family. I was surrounded by people who told me I was too young, too poor, too imperfect to become a teen parent. When my boyfriend took me to the

abortion facility, I ran out. I couldn't do it. I couldn't go through with the abortion. After two days of intense pressure my resolve crumbled and I went through with the abortion. I was 9 1/2 weeks pregnant. A few weeks after my abortion, consumed by intractable guilt, I tried to kill myself, but not long after that, I marched in Washington in support of abortion and soon after started volunteering as an escort at an abortion clinic. Eventually I was hired as a full-time employee.

"Since becoming pro-life, I've spent a lot of time thinking about why I took that job. In hindsight, I think I was trying to justify my role in the death of my child. By surrounding myself with people who all thought abortion was acceptable—even laudable—I was protecting my fragile psyche from more pain. I was young (in my late teens and early twenties) and I respected and admired my independent, intelligent, well-educated, and successful co-workers. If they all thought abortion was no big deal, maybe I should believe that as well, and stop torturing myself for being weak-willed and allowing my first child to be aborted.

"I did every job at that abortion facility apart from doctor and nurse. I started out answering phones and booking appointments. Later, I worked as a receptionist, checking in patients and taking payments. Soon I was trained to perform simple lab work including urine pregnancy tests and finger stick blood tests, to test iron levels. After that, I was taught medical assisting and took patients' blood pressure and pulse both before and after their abortions. I worked as a counselor in the recovery room, explaining aftercare and birth control. Then I was trained to counsel women before their abortions to obtain consent.

"When I was a pre-abortion counselor I would often visit my patients in the recovery room. I also

worked as a recovery room counselor. The facility where I worked performed abortions either awake with local anesthesia (injected directly into the cervix) or 'asleep' with intravenous sedation. These were done on different days of the week. On 'asleep' days patients spent an hour in the recovery room and were naturally groggy for the first 15-20 minutes or so. Once they came around the emotional reactions did not differ that much from the women who chose to be awake and have the abortion under local anesthetic. The majority were quiet and compliant, almost emotionless. Some were weepy, a few were belligerent.

"I also worked as an autoclave technician, scrubbing bloody surgical instruments after abortions. It was while working in the autoclave room that I began to have nightmares. The jars filled with the aftermath of the abortions were passed from the procedure rooms into the autoclave room through windows in the walls. The parts of the tiny bodies were reassembled on the countertop next to the sinks where I did dishes. I saw everything. I smelled everything. Then the nightmares started. Not just of missing my baby—that was common—but now I dreamt of all of the babies torn apart day after day at the abortion facility. It was then I spoke with the center's executive director to ask her if anyone else had nightmares after working in the autoclave room. She told me, 'What we do here is end a life. It's basic. If you aren't OK with that, you can't work here.' And after allowing me some days to think about it, I told her I was OK with it, and I kept my job. The nightmares decreased, but never went away completely. Even now.

"When I worked at the abortion clinic, the majority of my family and nearly all of my friends supported me; many admired me.

"I left my job at the abortion facility first in 1995 after graduating college to accept a job as a teen

crisis hotline counselor. Then I worked at the same abortion facility again part-time in 2002 after grad school, and only left to become a stay-at-home mother to my firstborn child. I remained pro-choice for eight years after leaving the abortion industry. I only became pro-life in November 2010 when learning of a gestational surrogate (a friend of a friend) who learned during prenatal testing that the baby she was carrying would be born with Down's Syndrome and the contracting (genetic) parents offered her payment of her contract in full to abort—and she did. This was my 'Ah-ha' moment. Children had become commodities to be created, bought, sold, and discarded at will—for 'quality control.' This was fundamentally wrong. Once I recognized that aborting a disabled baby for a cash payout was wrong, it wasn't too much of a leap for me to accept that all abortion was wrong. Babies in the womb possess intrinsic value and an inherent right to life."

Jules was surrounded by friends and family who were also pro-abortion and proud of her for the work she was doing. Notice that Jules was hired to answer phones and book appointments but eventually was taking blood pressure, doing urine tests and other things she had been not been properly trained for. This is a very common practice in the abortion industry. But Jules only began to have a problem with her job when she began seeing the remains of aborted babies. Still it took her several years to recognize that she was in danger of being swept under by the shockwaves of abortion.

Patricia Sandoval shared:

"I had three abortions before I went to work at Planned Parenthood in the Los Angeles area. The business performed about 40 abortions every week; 20 on Wednesday and 20 on Friday. My minimal training consisted of a very stern admonition to never call it a 'baby.' Never call it a 'he' or a 'she,'

instead say 'it' or a 'sac of tissue.' I was instructed to tell the women that I had had an abortion and was fine.

"My first job was to counsel women during their initial appointments, but on the first abortion day, I was told to accompany women during the abortion procedure itself. The first patient I accompanied was about three-and-a-half months pregnant. After the procedure, it was my job to take the bag containing the baby, tissue, and blood into a back room, dump out the contents onto a huge Petri dish and search for body parts. When I could identify all the parts, this brand new employee with very little training would declare the abortion complete.

"While examining the parts, I could clearly see the baby's knuckles, the hair on his legs, and his eyebrows and eyelashes.

"I could see the baby. It was seeing the humanity of the aborted baby that led me to quit my job at Planned Parenthood."

In all these cases it took several years for the abortion workers to gradually come out of the abortion industry, but for each of them, there was one event that created the "ah ha" moment that led them to leave the industry and seek healing.

If you would like to help someone you know leave the abortion industry please visit *www.SocietyofCenturions.com*. These individuals have been profoundly wounded and need deep healing. They need a helping hand to walk the difficult path of re-humanizing the children they killed by re-humanizing themselves. The Society of Centurions provides this path to healing, and each of these former abortion doctors and clinic staff need our prayers.

Chapter Eleven

Mourning the Lives
I Could Not Save

In this chapter we will examine the reality that every abortion impacts those who tried to stop it but couldn't. People who care about women and try to prevent abortions counsel pregnant moms in pregnancy centers, on the sidewalks in front of abortion facilities and elsewhere. Often, their efforts are in vain. These advocates for life also educate others, elect pro-life candidates, lobby to pass pro-life laws, and much more. Every time these efforts fail, lives are lost, and pro-life advocates need to mourn these losses. If they do not, they can end up carrying a burden of pain that, if not healed, can lead to bitterness or burnout.

Let's take a look at someone who works in a pregnancy resource center.

Evangeline works in a pregnancy help center in New Jersey, and her heart breaks every time an abortion-vulnerable woman goes through with an abortion. One loss, in particular, weighs heavily on her heart.

"A 19-year-old college student stopped into the center between classes. She already had had a pregnancy test and she wanted a second test for confirmation. It, too, was positive. This was a catastrophe for the woman, whose cultural background ensured that her future was mapped out for

her, and did not include a boyfriend from a different culture or a baby out of wedlock.

"Her mother ran the ship, and her life was completely planned out for her, The mother didn't even know that her daughter was seeing someone.

"The young woman said she hadn't menstruated in months, and an ultrasound she had at the center showed she was 20 weeks pregnant. She refused to look at the screen and we didn't want to force her, but she had her brother and (male) cousin come in to look, and I felt like they were assessing a crime scene and figuring out how they would clean it up.

"We convinced her to come back to show the ultrasound to her boyfriend, and they came in another day. Her boyfriend was excited about the pregnancy. He was in the military and he was ready to marry her. But the second time they came in, he had met her mother. I said, 'congratulations, you're going to be a dad,' and he said, 'we'll see.' He had met his girlfriend's mother, and she was poison. I was asking them what it would take for them to keep this baby, this precious, perfect baby we all saw on the ultrasound. I was trying to empower them. Her mother was the only obstacle.

"The young woman tried to tell her mother that she had been raped, but her mother saw through the lie. The mother made an appointment with a doctor and the young woman did not realize that her baby would die at that appointment.

"Her mother had totally tricked her. For me, there was a two-fold devastation. That baby, that big baby. I loved that baby. I just fell in love with that person who was torn to pieces. It was like I was watching someone drowning, and I couldn't save them. And for the mom, I almost wished we hadn't told her everything about the abortion procedure, because now she has to deal with knowing that.

"For me personally, it was very painful for many days, but gradually that pain turned into prayer. I'm not mad at the baby's mother, or at her mother. I'm mad at a doctor who could do that—rip this perfect baby to pieces. And I'm mad at our entire nation. How do we allow that?"

Evangeline's last contact with the young woman was through a text message: "Can I call you?" There was no reply.

Evangeline realizes she did everything possible to save that mom and baby from abortion, but the pressure the woman was receiving from her family and the culture she was raised in was too much. Evangeline also turned her anger towards the doctor, rightfully so, since he was the one who tore that baby apart. In order for a doctor to do an abortion like that, he has to dehumanize himself. Finally Evangeline reconciled the situation by turning to prayer.

In addition to individual prayer, we recommend that pregnancy centers have a periodic gathering of their counselors and volunteers for the purpose of sharing these experiences. Healing services also can help pregnancy center volunteers and staffers.

Like pregnancy center workers, sidewalk counselors also try to save babies and their moms from abortion. These counselors work on the front lines, right in front of the abortion clinics. I have been in front of abortion clinics all over the country, joining with the sidewalk counselors trying to save the life of a baby and also trying to protect the mom from the physical and psychological damage of abortion. Watching women going into an abortion business—with or without visible baby bumps—knowing they are about to destroy the life of that child, is very painful.

Let's meet Brian Gibson who has done sidewalk counseling work for decades, primarily in Minnesota.

Brian has been sidewalk counseling once or twice a week for more than 30 years, and as executive director of Pro-Life Action Ministries, he has trained thousands of others to stand outside abortion businesses and try to persuade mothers to choose life. His ministry is able to document almost 3,200 lives saved and he knows there have been many more.

"It's a joy that's hard to describe," Brian said of each saved baby. "We announce it to everyone, through email and social media. But it's God working through us to save those babies. It's a blessing from God when we are successful."

But the babies he and other counselors have not been able to save through their intervention weigh heavily on their hearts. "For me, it was more difficult earlier on," he said. "I would grieve. I would mourn. I would find myself getting depressed. You can go for weeks or months without a save that you know of. There was a lot of prayer at first with a lot of friends. I would get together weekly with a group of people and we would talk things out. I have burned out multiple times over the years, but you have to keep going. Children are still being killed."

When he is training sidewalk counselors, he makes sure they know they are not alone. "We want our sidewalk counselors to talk to us when they struggle. As part of the ongoing support we give them, we have an outreach coordinator who is in regular contact with them, and we try to get out and visit them while they are sidewalk counseling."

To guard against burnout and depression, Brian tells all those he trains that any sidewalk counselor needs good strong prayer support, and a good partner. "We warn people that this is tough and we tell them to get on their knees and pray because there are more failures than successes."

As he has grown in his own witness, he has begun to think differently about the babies he is not able to save.

It brings him some comfort to know that as they pass from this life to the next, someone still cared about them, someone was praying for them as they pass into eternity. "That brings me some comfort and solace. St. Teresa of Calcutta said our job isn't to be successful, it's to be faithful. Regardless of how worn out we may be, just the need and experience of being present keeps me going."

Brian did experience burnout over the years as the shockwaves of abortion shook the ground around his feet, but because of the many, many babies who were being killed by abortion he still felt a sense of urgency to press onward. He has, over the years, developed a very deep, spiritual prayer life and has incorporated it into his sidewalk counselor training program. To learn more about his ministry, Pro-life Action Ministries, visit *www.plam.org.*

Peter Breen has been a committed pro-life activist for decades. He and his wife Margie opened a pregnancy resource center shortly after their marriage. He now works as an attorney at the pro-life Thomas More Society in Chicago and serves as a representative in the Illinois General Assembly. He and his wife recently adopted a baby boy, so Peter has a unique and blessed perspective on things that are possible when a woman chooses life.

Peter acknowledged that there is a profound sense of loss when a baby can't be saved from abortion.

> *"At a pregnancy center, losing a baby to abortion is not uncommon, so you have to figure out how to cope with it. You feel terrible. It's like a punch to the gut, and as you try to make sense of it, you end up second-guessing yourself. 'Could we have been more articulate? Was there something we should have said, or something we shouldn't have said?' After awhile, you have to realize it's not about you—but you can't become numb to it. There's a middle place you have to get to.*
>
> *"For me, I believe you have to compartmentalize, but only temporarily. You have to step outside*

of the experience and give yourself some time to reflect and think on it. Then, you have the space you need to integrate the experience and the loss.

"Practically, that's not something you can do right away, because even though a particular mom may choose abortion, there's another mom waiting in the next room to discuss her pregnancy. For the sake of that mom, you have to keep going."

Peter's experience working in the pregnancy center—dealing with those tangible losses and finding that middle place—now gives him the determination to press on both on the legal and legislative front.

Preventing Burnout

More than 100,000 volunteers in the United States help to run weekend retreats offered by Rachel's Vineyard. During a retreat, the RV team actually relives the abortion experience with each person, according to Katie D'Annunzio, chief of operations.

"The Rachel's Vineyard teams relive the trauma, which can cause emotional havoc," Katie said. "There can be an aspect of burnout so we tell our retreat leaders that they have to prepare themselves emotionally and spiritually beforehand. We know that they are about to jump into the morass of each experience and deal with people who are broken, so they need to have their own spiritual lives in order to prepare for what's going to happen. Being overloaded with stories of such sadness takes its toll. After a retreat, we have a time of detoxification and prayer for the retreat leaders, and we ask God to lessen the impact of the trauma they have witnessed.

"But the joy and reward of the weekend process is that we get to see the transformation in the people who have attended. They are able to find a peace that they didn't have before and that's what prevents burnout in the retreat leaders. No matter what it does to us, it was worth the cost to see this healing happening before our eyes."

Katie said some retreat leaders have been working with Rachel's Vineyard for decades, and what makes them able to continue this emotional work is seeing the fruits of their labor—women and men released from the remorse and regret that had imprisoned them since the abortion.

"When we see the visible results," she said, "our faith becomes visible."

Let's meet Jody who is one of the Rachel's Vineyard retreat leaders.

Jody Duffy, a regional coordinator active with the Silent No More Awareness Campaign, has been a Rachel's Vineyard retreat leader since 2000 and is the director of Post Abortion Treatment & Healing (PATH) in Atlanta, Georgia. The sadness and trauma she deals with on a daily basis has not caused burnout yet. What's her secret?

"I have to take everything and bundle it up in a package and send it up to God and I tell Him, this is yours to deal with because I can't do it. My recharge is to constantly give to God the things I can't handle on my own.

"PATH volunteers dedicate up to an hour a week to prayer and make sure to pray—at least once a week—a prayer written by Father Richard Lopez:

"Lord Jesus, you came to show us the way home to the Father. We ask you to pour the power of Your grace into the minds and hearts of those in PATH who would show the path to healing for all those who suffer because of abortion. Set our hearts on fire with the love of your Sacred Heart so that no one we meet, crushed by pain, guilt, or grief will be beyond your saving touch. Awaken our minds to understand, touch our lips with your wisdom, and fill our hearts with such courage that no

attitude, no person, no situation will keep us from being your means of mercy."

Most volunteers at PATH have been there for ten years or longer, so clearly burnout is not an issue there. Jody says they come together as a group once or twice a year for a day of reflection.

"These days of recollection are good for us," Jody said. "They really help all of us recharge so we can be comforting and warm, receptive and loving to these women who are so deeply damaged."

These are just a few of the people who work in different aspects of the pro-life movement. There are many more whom I know personally, and they have been able to continue for decades without burnout because they have adopted a few general principles to keep one step ahead of the shockwaves of abortion:

• They practice their faith by attending Church on a regular basis and have a very strong prayer life.

• They take time to be with family and friends. Being a workaholic can lead to burnout very quickly.

• They realize that success is not measured by how many lives they save from abortion but rather that their efforts in speaking up for the unborn gives these tiny victims a voice.

Personally, I would like to add that in the almost three decades I have been doing this work, something that never fails to lift my spirits is my interaction with the people I have met who are also engaged in pro-life work. They give me so much encouragement, and I have made many lasting friendships over these years.

Remember, God does not require us to be successful, but He wants us always to be faithful! We are standing in the gap for these children and their moms.

Chapter 12

Abortion Scatters, Healing Gathers

In the 17th century, John Donne expressed in poetry a truth that this book expresses about the impact of abortion:

"No man is an island entire of itself; every man is a piece of the continent, a part of the main; if a clod be washed away by the sea, Europe is the less, as well as if a promontory were, as well as any manner of thy friends or of thine own were; any man's death diminishes me, because I am involved in mankind. And therefore never send to know for whom the bell tolls; it tolls for thee."

In the 20th century, Martin Luther King Jr. expressed it this way:

"In a real sense all life is inter-related. All men are caught in an inescapable network of mutuality, tied in a single garment of destiny. Whatever affects one directly, affects all indirectly. I can never be what I ought to be until you are what you ought to be, and you can never be what you ought to be until I am what I ought to be... This is the inter-related structure of reality" (Letter from a Birmingham Jail).

And in the current century, Pope Francis has emphasized this same theme multiple times in his encyclical letter on the environment, "Laudato Si." He writes, "Everything is related, and we human beings are united as brothers and sisters on a wonderful pilgrimage, woven together by the love God has for each of his creatures" (n. 92), and again, "Just as the different aspects of the planet—physical, chemical and biological—are interrelated, so too living species are part of a network which we will never fully explore and understand" (n. 138).

There is no such thing as a private abortion. Every abortion wounds us all, starting with family, friends, and practitioners, and reaching us who work to protect life. We all lose something, precisely because that child was meant to give something: to her family, to her friends, to her church and country. That child was meant to evoke from us the best of our love, and our relationships in the human family.

The abortion of that child is not just a loss as in the absence of what would have been in our lives; it is an act of violence, and a wound that damages the good that is already in our lives. As we have seen, it eats away at relationships, divides people from one another and from their best selves, and poisons the moral, social, and legal fabric of our world.

From the beginning, pro-abortion propaganda developed a mystique of an intimate privacy and secrecy around abortion with an emphasis on woman's personal decisions about her bodily autonomy. They speak of abortion as a personal and confidential healthcare decision about whether to accept or reject a pregnancy. They imagine that the enlightened, empowered woman facing an unplanned pregnancy steps away from the fray, looks calmly at her life situation, her goals for the future—and decides if a child can fit into that scenario.

As you can see by the language and concepts, this has the desired effect of establishing an impenetrable boundary around the woman who is discerning an abortion, or has experienced the procedure. This has proven to be a clever and very effective messaging campaign, which unconsciously has been absorbed by the majority of our fellow citizens. Even those who would not identify as "pro abortion" are uncomfortable interfering in what they see as a personal decision.

But in the real world, far from the pro-abortion spin, abortion is not experienced as an isolated autonomous decision of female empowerment—as if a pregnant woman is some sort of robot or isolated island. A host of people are often intimately involved and quite influential in a woman's decision to abort. Though often disconnected from each other, all those involved in the abortion decision and procedure remain deeply connected, emotionally and spiritually, to the child that dies in the womb.

A Transformation of Ministries

With almost 60 million abortions in our nation since 1973 and an expanded understanding of those directly impacted by the child's death, consider how far the shockwaves of abortion extend out into our families and communities.

However, in our doctors' and counseling offices, in our prayer groups and Bible studies . . . there is silence about abortion loss. In our workplaces, living rooms, and bedrooms . . . silence.

Not even our clergy and ministers, let alone family and friends feel comfortable talking about the subject. There is a general sense that by introducing this issue, even if in a non-condemning way, we are causing pain to those who have suffered this loss, shaming and judging them. We fear opening some kind of abortion Pandora's Box, unable to control the powerful forces unleashed. It's best to leave it alone. The mistaken but all too common pattern of a couple who, after the abortion procedure, never make mention of it again, has been adopted on a societal level.

But the personal, family, religious, and societal silence about abortion loss feeds the isolation of those who suffer. The person experiencing symptoms of complicated grief following abortion may not realize how these symptoms are connected to a past abortion procedure. This leads to considerable suffering not only for individuals; it can also affect marriage and family life, and directly impacts our schools and health-care systems.

The awareness of the shockwaves of abortion is essential to breaking this silence and transforming the ministries of the Church and the health care profession as well as wider social services. Take the example of Dr. Theresa Burke, for instance, who was jolted onto the path of studying the impact of abortion (and eventually founding Rachel's Vineyard Ministries) after she was told during her training not to even inquire as to the role abortion played in the eating disorders of the group she was counseling. It turns out that abortion indeed did impact most in that group.

We have seen how abortion is viewed as a very sensitive and private area of loss. While it certainly is sensitive, that doesn't mean it should be ignored. We know that other sensitive issues in our society (sexual abuse, breast cancer, spousal abuse, suicide) have been the subject of greater education of the public, and encouragement to reach out for help. And the public has benefited as a result.

Rachel's Vineyard, which has become the world's largest ministry of healing after abortion, and is a ministry of Priests for Life, utilizes a group retreat approach. People discuss their abortion, and what led to and followed it, in the confidential and supportive environment of a small group of women and men. This is not just to provide a "listening session;" this is rooted, rather, in the shockwaves of abortion, and the realization that as the wound is multifaceted and relational, so must the healing be. Nobody hurts from an abortion in isolation, and nobody heals in isolation. This is why Rachel's Vineyard also welcomes and serves more than the parents of the aborted baby. Other family members, friends, and former abortionists also come to grieve the loss of these children.

It is time to renew the ministries of healing after abortion. This renewal is based on the insights presented in this book, and the recognition that as the awareness grows of how multifaceted the wounds of abortion are, so must the healing ministries arise and equip themselves to embrace and guide the people who are discovering how wounded they are. The idea of "healing mothers and fathers" after abortion—and the training that goes with it—now needs to be amplified and expanded to include the many other groups of people and relationships that are hurt. The publicity, the wording, the marketing of the invitation to healing likewise have to adjust to encompass this much broader view of how abortion hurts and how we all heal.

And what also must be renewed in the process are the arenas of education, of preaching, and of politics.

The shockwaves of abortion on the survivors opens up a whole new dimension of education, one which is aware of the wounds of these students and particularly sensitive to showing them their inherent dignity and giving them confidence in the future. Religious education, in particular, needs to be alert to how the proclamation of the Son who died for us is most effectively made to youth who are hurting because a sibling died for them and they feel guilty for surviving and afraid of their parents.

The world of preaching therefore also takes on a new dimension with the shockwaves of abortion. We were created by the Word of God, and that same Word heals and redeems us. Preaching, which is a living encounter of the Word with the whole congregation, has a particularly urgent task today to help us all to see the shockwaves as they reverberate through our families and our society, and to take new hope and courage in walking the path of healing, all together.

Even the world of politics is affected. Understanding how the shockwaves destroys the myth of the "personal, private choice" creates a broader opening for addressing abortion in the political world and a broader motivation for the electorate to vote pro-life. After all, candidates and elected officials are committing themselves to serving the common good, which is very much at risk thanks to these multifaceted wounds caused by abortion.

Much of the effect of the abortion shockwaves, for better or for worse, is a dynamic that occurs on its own, and that the abortion supporters cannot stop. It is like the "dead end rule," which says that if you go down a dead end road and ignore the signs that say it's a dead end, you will soon learn by personal experience that it's a dead end. Just because someone ignores the signs that the Church and the pro-life movement put up saying abortion is harmful, doesn't mean they won't find out. In fact, they'll find out even if we put up no signs at all. And the dead end applies not just to the individual's experience, but that of all society.

Yet put up the signs we must, in order to spare as many as possible from going down the dead end road in the first place. And the Healing the Shockwaves initiative of the Silent No More Awareness Campaign (a joint project of Anglicans for Life and Priests for Life) provides an excellent game plan and tools to do that.

Healing the Shockwaves of Abortion (*Abortion Shockwaves.com*) provides a year-long campaign featuring:

• Education, resources, and testimonies on the web and in print/radio/social media that will focus each month on a specific group of people that are impacted in a special way by abortion loss.

• A nationwide call to accountability, repentance, and reconciliation

• A hope-filled invitation to healing.

• Web pages will have materials relevant to each month's topic, such as media talking points, press releases, position papers, preaching aids, and bulletin inserts for clergy/ministers.

• Interviews and testimonies with a message of education and healing will be spread though radio, television, and print—all promoted widely in various social media outlets to get the widest exposure possible.

You will find that if you make use of these tools, even people who have been fighting abortion for a long time will say things like, "I never thought of that before."

And one of the most exciting aspects of this activity consists of the gatherings of people who have been hurt by abortion in different ways, all testifying to their pain and healing. The Silent No More Awareness Campaign has done this extensively. At public rallies these people gather to hold their signs and to share publicly a brief testimony of their experience. Along with having women who say "I Regret My Abortion," along with having men who say "I Regret Lost Fatherhood," we have people holding signs saying "I Mourn My Aborted Sibling." We have people holding signs saying "I Regret Losing My Grandchild to Abortion." And we have people holding signs saying "I Regret Performing Abortions and Providing Abortions."

And as each person, wounded in a different way, expresses their own grief and repentance, this reinforces the repentance and healing of everyone else. What impact, for instance, do you think it makes on a mom who is resentful of her father for dragging her into an abortion clinic when, at one of these gatherings, she hears a dad publicly repent of having forced his daughter to have an abortion? And imagine how it helps a mom deal with her anger at the abortionist when a former abortionist is standing next to her at one of these gatherings apologizing publicly to all the women and families he has hurt by performing the procedure! Having all these people together creates a "kaleidoscope of healing," and shows in a visible, tangible way what a culture of life looks like.

The theme of these gatherings is very simple: Abortion hurts everybody. And because of that, we all heal together. One of the best things we can do is to spread the testimonies given at these gatherings.

Connecting the Dots

A key aspect of the healing of an individual after losing someone to abortion is the "connecting of the dots" between that abortion and subsequent problems the person experiences in life. An overprotective attitude toward a subsequent child, for example, or a drinking problem, or an inability to be intimate with a spouse, come into clearer focus when one realizes that a past abortion has led to or exacerbated that particular problem. And so it is with countless other problems as well—physical, emotional, interpersonal, and spiritual.

The awareness of the link between abortion and the problem does not, in and of itself, solve the problem, but it can give one a sense of more control over the problem and set into motion various steps of the process of overcoming it. Conquering the problem becomes more achievable as the healing from the abortion progresses.

Now if this is true in the healing journey of an individual, in relation to his or her own abortion, it stands to reason that we can also say that the healing of our entire society from so many of its wounds and conflicts, its confusions and fears, its failure in relationships and its self-destructive and addictive patterns of behavior, can progress in a more meaningful way as that society acknowledges that it has been damaged by abortion, and begins to discover the connection between those wounds and abortion.

Some 60 million legally permitted acts of child-killing do not constitute 60 million individual, isolated wounds. They constitute a multifaceted societal wound that we are only beginning to understand. And as society wrestles and struggles to find solutions to some of its most persistent and vexing problems, the silence surrounding abortion, and the unwillingness to name it and explore its devastating shockwaves, only delays progress in solving and even understanding those problems.

As Fr. Frank Pavone observed in his book, *Abolishing Abortion*:

"Soon after the December 2012 shooting in Sandy Hook Elementary School in Newtown, Connecticut, Dr. Keith Ablow of Fox News published an opinion piece titled "Who Would Kill Children?" He expressed, of course, the outrage of all but the most callous of our citizens that a shooting like this could occur. Even the abortion-supporting President Obama expressed his anger, lamenting the lost futures of these children. As to the question, though, of who would kill children, the answer is simple. We would. Twenty children were killed in Sandy Hook. On average, twenty unborn children are killed every day in the ten minutes it took Adam Lanza to kill those innocent kids in Connecticut. And we permit it."

Television commentator Melissa Harris-Perry, remarking on the controversial case of the slain teenager Trayvon Martin, observed that the verdict left the impression that it was "okay to kill an unarmed African American child who has committed no crime." Yet every day more than a thousand African American children are killed in the womb. Apparently it's more than an impression that this is "okay."

The shockwaves of abortion are not just among the smaller circles of family and friends we have identified. The shockwaves have extended as far as society itself extends.

As both spiritual and educational leaders have pointed out, the family is the basic cell of society. Healthy families lead to a healthy society, and broken families lead to a broken society. And as Dr. Philip Ney has said, nothing damages the family more than abortion. Nothing, therefore, damages society more than abortion.

The availability of abortion has also led to violence in the sense that when that legal door is open to mothers, it also increases the temptation of others to push them through it. Consider this quote: "We found that homicide was the leading cause of death among women who were pregnant—and accounted for 20% of deaths among that group, compared with 6% of deaths among non-pregnant women of reproductive age" (Isabelle Horon, Maryland Department of Health and Mental Hygiene, *Journal of the American Medical Association*, March 20, 2001).

Entire books are required just to list and briefly describe the studies that show the impact of abortion on societal health and well-being. *Detrimental Effects of Abortion: An Annotated Bibliography with Commentary*, Third Edition, edited by Thomas Strahan, is an excellent resource that has been available for some time, and a more recent and lengthier resource of the same type is *Complications: Abortion's Impact on Women*, from the deVeber Institute for Bioethics and Social Research. APART, the Alliance for Post-Abortion Research and Training (*StandApart.org*), provides similar information.

Family violence and child abuse are entire categories in the lists of studies of the impact of abortion, as is substance abuse, and as is psychiatric admissions of women following abortion. The wounds of so many millions, for so many decades, have to be treated. Our nation's healthcare and social services programs receive the shockwaves of abortion.

Then consider how the economy also receives those shockwaves. Laura Antkowiak, a research assistant for National Right to Life, published in that organization's newsletter in 2001 an excellent summary of the impact of abortion on the economy. She reminds us that pro-abortion arguments ignore the fact that most children become adults, and take their place in society as consumers, workers, innovators, and taxpayers. Economist Jacqueline Kasun finds that even an indigent child, over her lifetime, returns in taxes 3.7 times what was spent on her and her mother in cash, food, housing, and medical assistance. A whole body of research, facts and figures reinforces the message of common sense: An economy has lost something big when it has lost tens of millions of its people.

One of the reasons the abortion debate is so intractable is that people are torn between what they see as a choice between two good things: Helping the child, on the one hand, and helping the mom (and society) on the other. The more they see, however, that abortion helps neither the mom nor the society nor anyone else, then the conflict can be resolved in favor of life. The choice is not between "pro-life wins" or "pro-choice wins." In reality, either life wins or nobody wins. In short, one of the most important things we can do to stop abortion and heal its wounds is to keep asking the question, in discussions about various social ills, "How has abortion contributed to this problem?"

Conclusion

Come, Lord Jesus!

The Healing the Shockwaves of Abortion initiative looks at a different theme each month to help people focus on one or another of the ways abortion hurts people and their relationships. In the month of December, Christians observe the season of Advent and cry out, along with Scripture, "Come Lord Jesus!" The theme for Advent, which is also a theme for every day, is the coming of Jesus, to heal all the Shockwaves of Abortion. After eleven months of the Shockwaves initiative, and after the churches, the pro-life movement, and hopefully the nation have gained a much greater awareness of the multifaceted wounds of abortion, they will (and should) feel overwhelmed and more in need of help and salvation than ever before. This felt need for the Savior, for the Healer, leads the heart and mind to cry out, "Come, Lord Jesus!"

That cry expresses not only the need but also the hope: we have the certainty that there is One who can heal us. He has come to earth, and will come again, "with healing in his wings." Between his first and second comings, he comes in multiple ways through grace, through the presence of the Holy Spirit, and through the multiple healing programs which those who have been made aware of their wounds are urged to embrace.

The Lord who comes to heal us also unites us; that is, in fact, an integral aspect of the healing. Abortion divides. All sin divides; in fact, the word "diabolical" means "to split asunder." But Christ came "to destroy the works of the devil" (1Jn 3:8). As St. John remarks, Christ was to die "to gather into one all the scattered children of God" (John 11:52). Christ unites. Healing unites.

This is the unity of the family: we have found that we are children of God. We can cry out, "Abba," that is, "Father!" The Spirit Himself gives witness with our Spirit that we are children of God (see Rom 8:16).

Christ builds up the human family in himself, inviting all by his Word, uniting us in his Spirit, making us members of one Body. Abortion, in a reverse dynamic, says, "Go away! We have no room for you, no time for you, no desire for you, no responsibility for you. Get out of our way!" Abortion attacks the unity of the human family by splitting asunder the most fundamental relationship between any two persons: mother and child. Christ and his healing grace reverse the dynamic of abortion. Abortion scatters, healing gathers.

The importance of this theme reveals a key aspect and imperative of the entire Shockwaves initiative: to raise awareness of a wound requires developing resources to treat it. When one becomes aware of how wounded he or she is—in any of the groups that the initiative focuses on month after month—there is a fork in the road, a "crisis" in the classic sense of the word. At that point, one can either sink into despair, unconvinced that any healing is possible, or one can stand up, slowly and painfully, and with determination decide to begin the journey of healing.

When one decides to do the hard work necessary to heal, there is another fork in the road. One might think that this healing is just a human achievement: brute strength of will-power, or the power of the psychological sciences. Certainly we do need to utilize these human, natural elements. But it would be a fatal mistake to trust only in human beings, including ourselves, for healing. The proper road for the healing journey is marked by the awareness that we cannot do it without God and His grace. This leads to the cry of faith, "Come, Lord Jesus!"

At the same time, we avoid the mistake that some believers make when they think that because we have the saving grace of Jesus, we do not need the psychological sciences or the hard work of engaging in the grief process to heal the wounds of abortion. In fact, some will say that because they've accepted Jesus, who has forgiven them, they never have to think or talk about their abortion wounds again. This is a profound mistake, only reinforcing the isolation that the silent shame creates. Jesus' healing grace is real indeed, and it is precisely that grace that gives us the strength to engage in the hard work of the lifelong healing process.

Pro-life people are fond of quoting Deuteronomy 30:19, in which God says, "I have set before you life and death, the blessing and the curse. Choose life, then, that you and your descendants may live." Notice that while God gives his people freedom to choose the path they will follow, he does not give them the freedom to choose the consequences. If they choose life, blessings follow; if they choose death, curses follow. The lie of the culture of death is that you can choose not only the path but the consequences, and that somehow the choice of death can lead to blessings. But it cannot. And the consequences, as this verse and its context reveal, are for the whole community and for subsequent generations as well.

When we see the shockwaves of abortion, we see an empirical fulfillment of Deuteronomy 30. We see the multiple and intergenerational curses that accompany a personal and societal choice of abortion. And we see the multiple and intergenerational blessings of choosing life.

Yet in the end, it is not simply about information. It is about hope. The command to "choose life" is an arduous one, taking us well beyond ourselves, requiring us to give everything. Yet in that very command, God is telling us we have the power to fulfill it. Abortion is about despair. Choosing life is about hope; healing is about hope. And hope will not disappoint.

Please visit our website *www.abortionshockwaves.com.*

Afterword

By Georgette Forney, President of Anglicans for Life, Co-Founder of the Silent No More Awareness Campaign

I can still remember the summer day in 2014, when Fr. Frank Pavone, Janet Morana, and I were sitting in my family room discussing the phenomenal impact Kevin Burke's Turning the Hearts of the Fathers project had on the Silent No More Awareness Campaign's Father's Day outreach. It was during this discussion that the conversation took a turn that one can only describe as providential and is why this book exists.

As we acknowledged Kevin's comprehensive use of blogs, sermons, testimonies, prayers, and research to highlight the need for ministry for fathers dealing with abortion loss during the month of June, we asked ourselves collectively, are there other groups of people who would benefit from a similar effort? Were there other sets of people that were hurt, impacted, or changed after the abortion experience and death of the unborn baby that needed help to grieve and heal and forgive?

Already aware of Dr. Ney's outstanding research noted throughout this book, we realized the answer was yes, and we needed to create an initiative, building upon the foundation of the Silent No More Awareness Campaign. By extending awareness beyond the mother and father to the whole family, the extended family, community, and culture, we would be able to help people see the reality of the pain inflicted by abortion and also the power of healing, forgiveness, and restoration offered through Jesus Christ. We would also help the next generation recognize the destructive force that lies within abortion and highlight the consequences you avoid when you choose life.

You hold in your hands the culmination of our discussion in my family room and the planning, prayers, and preparation that began that day. The Healing the Shockwaves of Abortion initiative has been launched and now you can be part of the healing process. If you are hurting, visit *AbortionForgiveness.com* to find an abortion after-care program in your area. Share the information in this book. Buy extra copies of the book and share it with friends, neighbors, and family members. You never know who is suffering from an abortion experience, and your actions could open the door to their healing.

While I was helping with the final edit of the manuscript for this book, I once again encountered a real-life example of the Shockwaves of Abortion and was reminded about the importance of healing, especially within families.

As we came off the steps of Parliament Hill in Ottawa where women and men from the Silent No More Awareness Campaign had just given their testimonies as part of the March for Life in Canada, we were met by a woman sobbing uncontrollably. She literally fell into the arms of one of the speakers and could not stop crying. Canada's National Director, Angelina Steenstra, Janet, and I surrounded the two of them, praying for her while trying to comfort her.

She finally calmed down enough to stammer out her story as big tears continued to fall down her cheeks. She explained that her sister had an abortion because the child had been diagnosed with a cleft palate, a facial and oral malformation.

I remember thinking as she was talking, "This is another example of a relative experiencing the shockwaves of an abortion." But as she went on, she explained to us that she had also been born with a cleft palate and, when her sister aborted the baby, it felt as though her sister was rejecting her and wishing she had not been born as well.

She began sobbing all over again as she asked why children with this correctable disability in a country with the medical resources available had to die. Why did their parents and family reject them because they were less than perfect?

Not only was she grieving the unnecessary death of her nephew or niece, she was mourning for all the children who could have and should have been given the same corrective surgeries she went through. For her, every child aborted because they were diagnosed in utero with some type of physical ailment was seen by her as a rejection of her personhood. Their abortion called into question her dignity, existence, and right to be alive.

I realized we were blessed to meet this very coura-geous woman who chose to be vulnerable and to come to us knowing we would understand her grief. We all, unfortunately, had in common the loss of family mem-bers to abortion. But her level of grief and pain was deeply rooted and personal in a unique way.

Based on Dr. Ney's descriptions of the various types of survivors explained in Chapter 8, it was clear that this young woman was someone who identified as a Disabled Survivor. Did she wonder if her parents would have aborted her if they knew she would be born with a cleft palate?

I also wondered about her relationship with her sister. Will their relationship be able to heal? As they not only need to address the grief due to the loss of the aborted child, but the implied rejection that now stands between the two women.

As Janet noted, abortion scatters hearts and relationships, but healing gathers and brings people back together. Will these two women be able to reconcile? Will their mutual pain bring them together or further widen the divide between them even though they are sisters?

This encounter reinforced for me the importance of addressing not only the epicenter of the earthquake (the abortion) with the mother, baby, father, and abortionist but the aftershocks, the reverberations that may be far less visible but just as damaging to family members, friends, and our culture in general.

When the seven Supreme Court justices made the decision to legalize abortion back in 1973, I am sure they never considered or imagined the consequences and shockwaves Roe vs. Wade would trigger. But now that we know and see that vast number of casualities beyond the dead baby that are devastated by abortion, may we be inspired to do all we can to end abortion and put an end to the growing number of people wounded by the shockwaves of abortion.

Help us build awareness so that together we can heal the hearts of those grieving the death of aborted children and make abortion unthinkable and unnecessary.

Visit *AbortionShockwaves.com* and *SilentNoMore.com* for more information.

Important Websites

Priests for Life
www.priestsforlife.org

Silent No More
www.silentnomore.com

Abortion Shockwaves
www.abortionshockwaves.com

Rachel's Vineyard
www.rachelsvineyard.org

Dr. Philip Ney
www.messengers2.com

Abortion survivors
www.abortionsurvivors.com

Abortion Pill Reversal
www.abortionpillreversal.com

Society of Centurions
www.societyofcenturions.com

Abortion Forgiveness
www.abortionforgiveness.com

Operation Rescue
www.operationrescue.org

40 Days for Life
www.40daysforlife.com

Americans United for Life
www.aul.org

National Right to Life
www.nrlc.org

American Associations of Pro-life OB/Gyns
www.aaplog.org

Post Abortion Treatment and Healing
www.healingafterabortion.org

JANET A. MORANA serves as the Executive Director of Priests for Life and the Co-Founder of the Silent No More Awareness Campaign, the world's largest mobilization of women and men who have lost children to abortion.

Mrs. Morana was born in Brooklyn, NY. She holds a degree in foreign languages and a Masters degree in Education, as well as a Professional Diploma in Reading from St. John's University, graduating with several awards for academic excellence. For eleven years, Mrs. Morana served as a full-time public school teacher in Staten Island, New York. During that time, she spearheaded numerous literacy, science, cultural and educational programs, and won many awards and financial grants for her school district.

Since 1989, Mrs. Morana has held various local and national leadership roles in the pro-life movement. She served on the board of the Staten Island Right to Life Committee. She ran for the New York City Council on the Right-to-Life Line and received the largest percentage of votes of any Right to Life candidate in the Party's history.

She has traveled extensively throughout the country and the world, giving pro-life training seminars for clergy and laity, including at Pontifical universities in Rome, and representing Priests for Life at national and international pro-life conferences. She has helped coordinate relationships between pro-life organizations and the Vatican as well as the White House.

She is featured on Fr. Pavone's *Defending Life* television series on EWTN. She is the Co-host of *The Catholic View for Women* also seen on EWTN. She is a weekly guest on EWTN Global Catholic Radio with Teresa Tomeo, has appeared on Fox News Channel and numerous other media outlets. She is the co-founder of the *Silent No More Awareness Campaign*, an international effort to assist women who have had abortions to share their testimonies. In 2003 she addressed the Pro-Life Caucus of the U.S. House of Representatives on life issues. In 2009 the international Legatus organization bestowed upon her the Cardinal John O'Connor Pro-life Hall of Fame Award. She is the author of *Recall Abortion* published by Saint Benedict Press in 2013.

To arrange a media interview, email: media@priestsforlife.org
or call 347-286-7277

To invite Mrs. Morana to speak in your area, contact our Speakers Bureau at 321-500-1000 Email: travels@priestsforlife.org

Acknowledgments

This book would not have been possible without the decades of research and the wisdom of Dr. Philip Ney, a close friend and colleague in pro-life for more than 20 years. Through his Hope Alive counseling program, he has pioneered healing not just for women and men harmed by abortion, but for whole families. His work provided the foundation for this book, and the Holy Spirit provided the inspiration.

I am very grateful to my colleagues in the Silent No More Awareness Campaign: co-founder Georgette Forney of Anglicans for Life, Father Frank Pavone, our Pastoral Director, and Kevin Burke, LSW, co-founder of Rachel's Vineyard and a pastoral associate of Priests for Life. When Fr. Frank, Georgette, and I began discussing the damage abortion causes to many groups of people, it led to the Healing the Shockwaves of Abortion initiative that we kicked off in 2015.

I would also like to acknowledge and thank Anthony DeStefano and literary manager Peter Miller for working so hard to get this book in the right hands. Thank you to Leslie Palma-Simoncek, my research assistant and friend. Thank you to Emilie Cerar, my editor at Catholic Book Publishing.

Thank you, finally, to the women, men, and families of the Silent No More Awareness Campaign, whose courage and commitment to protecting the unborn is unmatched. If you did not step out in faith to tell the stories of your abortion experiences and the deep regret that followed, countless others who have made that choice would remain locked in a prison of shame and guilt. You are truly healing the world.

By Janet Morana

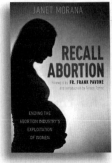

"Recall Abortion manages to go beyond the headlines in the abortion war to tell the truth about this terrible product."

—Joe Scheidler, Pro-Life Action League

"For decades I have been working to reverse this tragic decision that was made in my name. Janet Morana's recall effort might be the way to finally end the catastrophe of abortion."

—Norma McCorvey, Jane Roe of Roe v. Wade (1947-2017).

Available at www.recallabortion.com
Hardcover **15.00**
Paperback **10.00**

By Fr. Frank Pavone

PRO-LIFE REFLECTIONS FOR EVERY DAY — By Fr. Frank Pavone. Contains a text from Scripture and other Church documents, a reflection and a prayer intended for pro-life believers to help build and strengthen the Culture of Life. 192 pages. Size 4 x 6¼.
No. 168/19—Dura-Lux cover **8.95**
ISBN 978-0-89942-168-1

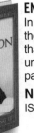

ENDING ABORTION — By Fr. Frank Pavone. In a collection of stirring and informative pro-life essays, the author convincingly portrays the negative ramifications that the abuse of freedom and the right to choose have unleashed on our society since abortion was legalized. 224 pages. Size 5½ x 8¼.
No. 939/04—Flexible cover **9.95**
ISBN 978-0-89942-131-5

Available at www.catholicbookpublishing.com